"FEAR is the tool of a man-made devil. Self-confident faith in one's self is both the man-made weapon which defeats this devil and the man-made tool which builds a triumphant life. And it is more than that. It is a link to the irresistible forces of the universe which stand behind a man who does not believe in failure and defeat as being anything but temporary experiences."

—NAPOLEON HILL

Praise for Napoleon Hill's
OUTWITTING THE DEVIL

"*Outwitting the Devil* proves once again that the messages and philosophies of Napoleon Hill are timeless. This book contains insights on how to break free of habits and attitudes that prevent success and will ultimately lead to happiness and prosperity. If you want to break through your own road blocks, read this book!"

—T. HARV EKER, author of #1 *New York Times* best-seller *Secrets of the Millionaire Mind*

"If you want to own your life, you have to own your money. In *Outwitting the Devil*, Napoleon Hill shares what may be holding you back in your financial life, and charts the course for you to take control and own the life of your dreams."

—JEAN CHATZKY, Financial Journalist and author of *The Difference: How Anyone Can Prosper in Even the Toughest Times*

"I have probably studied Napoleon Hill's work as much as anyone alive. It was 50 years ago that I picked up *Think and Grow Rich*. I have it with me all the time and read it every day. When Sharon Lechter sent me a copy of *Outwitting the Devil* I thought he has done it again, another world changer. This book is going to eliminate the spiritual confusion people worldwide are presently experiencing, and it will tear down the wall of ignorance that separates millions of individuals from the freedom their soul is seeking."

—BOB PROCTOR, founder of Life Success, www.bobproctor.com

"Most people will achieve their greatest success one step beyond what looked like their greatest failure. While Napoleon Hill's *Think and Grow Rich* provided a roadmap to success, *Outwitting the Devil* will help you break through the barriers that may be holding you back."

—BRAIN TRACY, author of *The Way to Wealth*

"The story *behind* this story is amazing in and of itself, being previously unpublished for more than seventy years. Now, the fact that this book is finally being released at a time when its message is potentially even more relevant than it was when it was originally written is a testament to Napoleon Hill's timeless mastery of human potential."

—IVAN MISNER, PhD, *New York Times* best-selling author and founder of BNI®

"The world's economic status has created a situation of no energy in people's conversations. Napoleon Hill's *Outwitting the Devil* is a roadmap on how to change the conversation to a positive, empowering conversation. This book will help you shift from no energy to Yes! Energy and start to change your life for the better."

—LORAL LANGEMEIER, five-time best-selling author, speaker, and coach

"Diversity is a wonderful thing. But, at our core we are all still human beings. And most of the time we simply don't stray from human nature. Napoleon Hill's *Outwitting the Devil* is undeniable proof that his work is STILL relevant today and transcends ALL generations."

—TR GARLAND, #1 best-selling author of *Building the Ultimate Network*

"As the devilish dialogue progresses, Satanic schemes and tricks are revealed, while Hill's own observations on success, failure, and human behavior emerge. Many readers will find that Hill's writings still remain relevant today."

—*PUBLISHERS WEEKLY*

"I couldn't help but think that these points are still so relevant today in our own recovering economy, even though they were written during a similar challenge over 70 years ago. I guess we all should take comfort in the fact that even though we live in a world of constant change, some things about human nature will always be the same. Can you outwit the Devil today to succeed in your dream?"

—MARTIN ZWILLING, Forbes.com

"*Outwitting the Devil* is a timeless primer on overcoming fear, self-doubt and, other internal leadership challenges. If you liked Hill's classic, *Think and Grow Rich, Outwitting the Devil* is a must-have addition to your business bookshelf."

—GAEBLER.COM

Napoleon Hill

OUTWITTING THE DEVIL

The Secret to Freedom and Success

Annotated by

SHARON LECHTER

with The Napoleon Hill Foundation

STERLING
New York

An Imprint of Sterling Publishing
387 Park Avenue South
New York, NY 10016

STERLING and the distinctive Sterling logo are registered trademarks of Sterling Publishing Co., Inc.

For further reading, please visit:
www.naphill.com
www.outwittingthedevil.com
www.sharonlechter.com

ISBN 978-1-4549-0067-2

Distributed in Canada by Sterling Publishing
c/o Canadian Manda Group, 165 Dufferin Street
Toronto, Ontario, Canada M6K 3H6
Distributed in the United Kingdom by GMC Distribution Services
Castle Place, 166 High Street, Lewes, East Sussex, England BN7 1XU
Distributed in Australia by Capricorn Link (Australia) Pty. Ltd.
P.O. Box 704, Windsor, NSW 2756, Australia

For information about custom editions, special sales, and premium and corporate purchases, please contact Sterling Special Sales at 800-805-5489 or specialsales@sterlingpublishing.com.

Manufactured in the United States of America

4 6 8 10 9 7 5 3

www.sterlingpublishing.com

CONTENTS

Note to Readers by Sharon Lechter xi
Foreword by Mark Victor Hansen xv

Chapter 1 My First Meeting with Andrew Carnegie 1
Chapter 2 A New World Is Revealed to Me 31
Chapter 3 A Strange Interview with the Devil 51
Chapter 4 Drifting with the Devil 71
Chapter 5 The Confession Continues 97
Chapter 6 Hypnotic Rhythm 119
Chapter 7 Seeds of Fear 139
Chapter 8 Definiteness of Purpose 147
Chapter 9 Education and Religion 159
Chapter 10 Self-Discipline 185
Chapter 11 Learning from Adversity 201
Chapter 12 Environment, Time, Harmony, and Caution 219
Summary 243

Afterword by Michael Bernard Beckwith 252
In Reflection by Sharon Lechter 255
Acknowledgments 259
About the Authors 260
Index 262
About The Napoleon Hill Foundation 268
Share Your Stories 269

Portrait of a young Napoleon Hill

RIGHT: *The introduction, typed on a manual typewriter with handwritten notes, from the original manuscript by Napoleon Hill.*

OUTWITTING the DEVIL!

BY THE MAN WHO BROKE THE DEVIL'S CODE AND FORCED HIM TO CONFESS.

The Secret of how the Author Attained Physical and Financial Freedom

* * * * * * * *** *

The <u>boldest</u> and the most inspiring of the self-help books by America's number one success philosopher who, after thirty years of diligent snooping, found the Devil and wrung from him an astounding confession disclosing where he lives, why he exists, and how he gains control over the minds of people, <u>and how anyone can outwit him</u>. The book is a generous course in psychology, making clear the working principles of the human mind. When you finish this story of the Devil you will know much more about God.

* * * * * * *

By

Napoleon Hill

author of

and

THINK AND GROW RICH

MASTER-KEY TO RICHES

NOTE TO READERS

by
SHARON LECHTER

OUTWITTING THE DEVIL is the most profound book I have ever read.

First, I was incredibly honored when Don Green, CEO of the Napoleon Hill Foundation, trusted me enough to ask me to become involved in this project. And then I read the manuscript! I couldn't sleep for a week.

Written on a manual typewriter in 1938 by the Master himself, Napoleon Hill, this manuscript had been locked away and hidden by Hill's family for seventy-two years. Why? Because they were frightened by the response it would invoke. Hill's courage in revealing the Devil's work around each of us every day, in our churches, our schools, and our politics, threatened the very core of society as it was known at the time.

When asked why the family had hidden the manuscript, Don Green recites the following inside story:

> It was the objections of Hill's wife, Annie Lou. She was secretary to Dr. William Plumer Jacobs, president of Presbyterian College in Clinton, South Carolina. Jacobs was also owner of Jacobs Press and a public counselor to a group of South Carolina textile firms. Jacobs hired Hill to come to Clinton to work for him, and Annie Lou did not want the book published because of the role of the Devil. She feared the response from organized religion (and maybe for Hill's job). Even though Hill died in 1970, Annie Lou did not die until 1984. Upon Annie Lou's death, the manuscript

> came into the possession of Dr. Charlie Johnson, then the president of the Napoleon Hill Foundation. Charlie was the nephew of Annie Lou Hill. Charlie's wife, Frankie, knew and shared Annie Lou's feelings. Frankie told Charlie that she did not want the article published while she was alive either. Charlie's wife passed away a couple of years ago and Charlie finally gave me the manuscript, bound in red leather and embossed with the letters *Outwitting the Devil* in gold on the cover. The Foundation believes the manuscript has a powerful message that needs to be shared.

After speaking with Don, I was overcome with a powerful realization. This book, even though written in 1938, was actually meant to be published today . . . meant to rock our society today! It was intended to provide answers during this uncertain economic and spiritual time. It provides the keys for each of us to outwit the Devil in our own lives. It shows us how to chart a course for success and to add value to the world around us through the process.

Just as *Think and Grow Rich* helped us recover and succeed after the Great Depression, *Outwitting the Devil* was written to help each of us recover and succeed today!

You may ask if Hill believes his conversation with the Devil was real, or was it merely imaginary? The choice is yours. But I also asked Don Green about Hill's thoughts in his other writings to see if we could get another look inside Hill's head. Don's response was as follows:

> The use of imaginary conversations was not new to Hill. In 1953, Hill published *How to Raise Your Own Salary*, which was written as a conversation between Hill and Carnegie. Hill had actually interviewed Carnegie in 1908 and Carnegie died in 1919, well before its publication.

> This was not the first time Hill used imaginary meetings to convey what he was writing about. In *Think and Grow Rich*, Hill, writing about the sixth sense, wrote about his imaginary council meeting with the nine men whose lifeworks had been the most impressive to Hill. These nine imaginary council members were Emerson, Paine, Edison, Darwin, Lincoln, Burbank, Napoleon, Ford, and Carnegie.
>
> Hill wrote in *Think and Grow Rich* that during his meetings with his "Invisible Counselors" he found his mind most receptive to ideas, thoughts, and knowledge that reached him during these times when his sixth sense was activated.
>
> *Outwitting the Devil* was by no means his first time to write about religion. In fact, after he published *Law of Success* in 1928, he received letters of criticism about his stance on schools and religion. In *Think and Grow Rich*, in the chapter titled "The Six Ghosts of Fear," Hill wrote that fear of death, in the majority of cases, could be charged to religious fanaticism. Hill had much to say about religious leaders in this section of his classic best seller.
>
> Hill had much to say about religion even in his *Hill's Golden Rule Magazine*. He wrote an article, "A Suggestion to Ministers of the Gospel," in which he admonished church leaders to teach their followers to practice harmony among each other.

So the choice is yours. Did Hill actually talk to the Devil or is this a parable created to reach and touch your heart? Hill's unique style will pull you in and move you in ways you never thought possible. The words in this book are Hill's own. Since the original manuscript was quite lengthy, I edited with careful precision to preserve the profound impact of his message.

I have kept his original language in place even when modern grammar may have dictated adjustments.

In an effort to highlight certain issues, bring clarity to his words, and show how his predictions have become realities, I have added my thoughts throughout the manuscript in a different type style. This allows you to choose to read the book either with my comments or without.

Please enjoy this powerful book and share it with your friends and family. The power in Hill's words can and will change your life.

FOREWORD

Dr. Napoleon Hill is arguably the most famous self-help action writer, thinker, évocateur, and best-selling author of all time. We ask that you refer quickly to the actual interview with the Devil. You will thus get the impact in your life of who the Devil really is and what he does to 98 percent of living beings, according to the Devil himself.

As a thought stimulator, Hill quickly starts the book's journey, taking us through his life and what was meaningful and life-changing to him. Hill learned the greatest and most useful and instantly helpful success principles on the planet, but he did not know how to use and easily apply them. We predict that this is true for many people still today. It is easy to say the words and sometimes even think the thoughts. It takes a profound and lasting decision to actually live by the principles daily in every way. Sharon Lechter illuminates what Hill's words mean when transported into today's dollars, thinking, and understanding.

Dr. Hill's goal was to communicate clearly a philosophy and practice of individual achievement that would stimulate lasting happiness. His inner knower guided him to find his own life's rainbow.

You are being tested now in the toughest times imaginable, just as Hill was during the Depression. He felt, acted, and became depressed and despondent, an attitude that was deleterious to his very beingness, just as it is to you and your wellness. Reading this inspiring book can help you snap out of your lethargy and negative-mindedness and get you on a new and more glorious path to an ever brighter, better, and more rewarding future.

Like Hill, you are here to master your fears and not let them master you, to live passionately and with purpose, to decide what you want to be, do, and have, and to make it so.

As you rediscover the marvelous and magical discoveries of Dr. Hill, you will know and believe that you can match them and surpass them if you want to, because you are unlimited. Hill correctly says, "Your only limitations are self-imposed." This book will help you be aware that you can achieve your breakthroughs using all that he learned by interviewing the five hundred greatest living achievers.

You will discover whether the Devil he interviews is real or imaginary, much like the Devil that you may personally be dealing with in your life and experience.

—MARK VICTOR HANSEN

MARK VICTOR HANSEN is co-creator of the #1 *New York Times* best-selling series *Chicken Soup for The Soul®* and co-author of *Cracking the Millionaire Code*, *The One Minute Millionaire*, and *Cash in a Flash*.

· *Chapter One* ·

MY FIRST MEETING WITH ANDREW CARNEGIE

FOR MORE THAN A QUARTER OF A CENTURY my major purpose has been that of isolating and organizing into a philosophy of achievement the causes of both failure and success, with the object of being helpful to others who have neither the inclination nor the opportunity to engage in this form of research.

My labor began in 1908, as the result of an interview that I had with the late Andrew Carnegie. I frankly told Mr. Carnegie that I wished to enter law school and that I had conceived the idea of paying my way through school by interviewing successful men and women, finding out how they came by their success, and writing stories of my discoveries for magazines. At the end of our first visit Mr. Carnegie asked whether or not I possessed enough courage to carry out a suggestion he wished to offer me. I replied that courage was about all I did have and that I was prepared to do my best to carry out any suggestion he cared to offer.

He then said, "Your idea of writing stories about men and women who are successful is commendable, as far as it goes, and I have no intention of trying to discourage you from carrying out your purpose, but I must tell you that if you wish to be of enduring service, not only to those now living, but to posterity as well, you can do so if you will take the time to organize all of the causes of failure as well as all of the causes of success.

"There are millions of people in the world who have not the slightest conception of the causes of success and failure. The schools and colleges teach practically everything except the principles of individual achievement. They require young men and women to spend from four to eight years acquiring abstract knowledge, but do not teach them what to do with this knowledge after they get it.

"The world is in need of a practical, understandable philosophy of achievement, organized from the factual knowledge gained from the experience of men and women in the great university of life. In the entire field of philosophy I find nothing which even remotely resembles the sort of philosophy which I have in mind. We have few philosophers who are capable of teaching men and women the art of living.

"It seems to me that here is an opportunity which should challenge an ambitious young man of your type; but ambition alone is not enough for this task which I have suggested. The one who undertakes it must have courage and tenacity.

"The job will require at least twenty years of continuous effort, during which the one who undertakes it will have to earn his living from some other source, because this sort of research is never profitable at the outset, and generally those who have contributed to civilization through work of this nature have had to wait a hundred years or so after their own funerals to receive recognition for their labor."

NOTE to READERS: Sharon Lechter adds her comments in special sections like this.

Twenty years of labor with no pay and possibly no recognition! How would you respond to this "offer"? As he discusses below, Hill accepted Carnegie's challenge and, with a letter of introduction from Carnegie, set about interviewing the giants of that time, including Theodore Roosevelt, Thomas Edison, John D. Rockefeller, Henry Ford, Alexander Graham Bell, King Gillette (founder of the Gillette Safety Razor Company), and many others. His effort ultimately culminated in the publication of several books, including the eight-volume *Law of Success* and *Think and Grow Rich* after more than twenty-five years of research. *Think and Grow Rich* is widely recognized as

the seminal work in self-development, introducing essentially all the principles that continue to serve as the foundation for the teachings of the personal development gurus of today. As reflected in Hill's own description, the process of developing and publishing *Think and Grow Rich* was itself a study in the principles he revealed. It may be telling that the manuscript of *Outwitting the Devil* was written the year after *Think and Grow Rich* was published, since this work may reveal the frustration and revelation of Hill's "other self" and how he conquered his frustrations and succeeded in using the very principles he described in *Think and Grow Rich*. *Outwitting the Devil* will reveal Hill's spiritual awakening and how each of us can learn from his encounter with the Devil.

"If you undertake this job, you should interview not only the few who have succeeded, but the many who have failed. You should carefully analyze many thousands of people who have been classed as 'failures,' and I mean by the term 'failures,' men and women who come to the closing chapter of life disappointed because they did not attain the goal which they had set their hearts upon achieving. As inconsistent as it may seem, you will learn more about how to succeed from the failures than you will from the so-called successes. They will teach you what not to do.

"Along toward the end of your labor, if you carry it through successfully, you will make a discovery which may be a great surprise to you. You will discover that the cause of success is not something separate and apart from the man; that it is a force so intangible in nature that the majority of men never recognize it; a force which might be properly called the 'other self.' Noteworthy is the fact that this 'other self' seldom exerts its influence or makes itself known excepting at times of unusual emergency, when men are forced, through adversity and temporary defeat, to change their habits and to think their way out of difficulty.

"My experience has taught me that a man is never quite so near success as when that which he calls 'failure' has overtaken him, for it is on occasions of this sort that he is forced to think. If he thinks accurately, and with persistence, he discovers that so-called failure usually is nothing more than a signal to re-arm himself with a new plan or purpose. Most real failures are due to limitations which men set up in their own minds. If they had the courage to go one step further, they would discover their error."

"Most real failures are due to limitations which men set up in their own minds."

A negative mind-set and self-doubt can be the primary obstacle to success. With the current economic downturn, far too many people who have, all their life, done everything right are now, for the first time, facing severe economic adversity. The greatest barrier to their recovery is their own fear and self-doubt instilled by their recent experience. Have you allowed the current economic downturn to overtake you? Have self-doubt and self-sabotage held you back from reaching your dreams? Are you your own worst enemy? In *Think and Grow Rich*, Hill told the story of R.U. Darby, a gold prospector. Frustrated when a rich vein of gold apparently ran out, Darby sold his gold claim for

a pittance to the town junkman. The junkman brought in the right expert advisers and found that Darby would have rediscovered the vein—had he moved his digging by a mere three feet. Had Darby persevered he would have made his fortune, but he gave up and abandoned his dreams—when he was only three feet from gold. Rather than being crushed by his error, Darby learned from his experience and went on to build an insurance empire. Will you abandon your quest just before reaching great success, when you are only three feet from gold? (You can read how many of today's icons persevered through difficult situations in the book *Three Feet from Gold*.)

Begin Life Anew

Mr. Carnegie's speech reshaped my entire life and planted in my mind a burning purpose, which has driven me ceaselessly, and this despite the fact that I had but a vague idea as to what he meant by the term "other self."

During my labor of research into the causes of failure and success I have had the privilege of analyzing more than 25,000 men and women who were rated as "failures," and over 500 who were classed as "successful." Many years ago I caught my first glimpse of that "other self" Mr. Carnegie had mentioned. The discovery came, as he said it would, as the result of two major turning-points of my life, which constituted emergencies that forced me to think my way out of difficulties such as I had never before experienced.

I wish it were possible to describe this discovery without the use of the personal pronoun, but this is impossible because it came through personal experiences from which it cannot be separated. To give you the complete picture I shall have to go back to the first of these two major turning-points and bring you up to the discovery step by step.

The research necessary for the accumulation of the data, from which the seventeen principles of achievement and the thirty major causes of failure were organized, required years of labor.

I had reached the false conclusion that my task of organizing a complete philosophy of personal achievement had been completed. Far from having been completed, my work had merely begun. I had erected the skeleton of a philosophy by organizing the seventeen principles of achievement and the thirty major causes of failure, but that skeleton had to be covered with the flesh of application and experience. Moreover, it had to be given a soul through which it might inspire men and women to meet obstacles without going down under them.

The "soul," which had yet to be added, as I discovered later, became available only after my "other self" made its appearance, through two major turning-points of my life.

Resolving to turn my attention, and whatever talents I might possess, into monetary returns through business and professional channels, I decided to go into the profession of advertising, and I became the advertising manager of the LaSalle Extension University of Chicago. Everything went along beautifully for one year, at the end of which I was seized by a violent dislike for my job and resigned.

I then entered the chain store business, with the former president of the LaSalle Extension University, and became the president of the Betsy Ross Candy Company. Unfortunate—or what seemed to me at the time to be unfortunate—disagreements with business associates disengaged me from that undertaking.

The lure of advertising still was in my blood, and I tried again to give expression to it by organizing a school of advertising and salesmanship, as a part of Bryant & Stratton Business College.

The enterprise was sailing smoothly and we were making money rapidly when the United States entered World War I. In response to an inner urge which no words can describe, I walked away from the school and entered the service of the United States government, under President Woodrow Wilson's personal direction, leaving a perfectly sound business to disintegrate.

On Armistice Day 1918, I began the publication of *The Golden Rule* magazine. Despite the fact that I did not have a penny of capital, the magazine grew rapidly and soon gained a nation-wide circulation of nearly half a million, ending its first year's business with a profit of $3,156.

For a proper perspective, $3,156 in 1918 would represent $45,000 today based on the Consumer Price Index average for each year compiled by the U.S. Bureau of Labor Statistics and $202,000 using the nominal GDP per capita tables. Not a bad profit for a first year in the magazine business . . . when 80 to 90 percent of new titles fail and even the successful ones take three to five years to become profitable (http://www.magazinepublisher.com/startup.html).

Some years later I learned, from an experienced publisher, that no man experienced in the publication and distribution of national magazines would think of starting such a magazine with less than half a million dollars of capital.

The Golden Rule magazine and I were destined to part company. The more we succeeded the more discontented I became, until finally, due to an accumulation of petty annoyances caused by business associates, I made them a present of the magazine and stepped out. Through that move perhaps I tossed a small fortune over my shoulder.

This was only the beginning of Hill's love for magazines. *The Golden Rule* was followed by his publication of *The Napoleon Hill Magazine*. Later in life he became the editor of *SUCCESS*, a magazine that is still published today.

Next I organized a training school for salesmen. My first assignment was to train a sales army of 3,000 people for a chain store company, for which I received $10 for each salesman who went through my classes. Within six months my work had netted me a little over $30,000. Success, as far as money was concerned, was crowning my efforts with abundance. Again I became "fidgety" inside. I was not happy. It became more obvious every day that no amount of money would ever make me happy.

Without the slightest reasonable excuse for my actions, I stepped out and gave up a business from which I might easily have earned a healthy salary. My friends and business associates thought I was crazy, and they were not backward about saying so.

Frankly, I was inclined to agree with them, but there seemed nothing I could do about it. I was seeking happiness and I had not found it. At least that is the only explanation I could offer for my unusual actions. What man really knows himself?

"Again I became 'fidgety' inside. I was not happy. It became more obvious every day that no amount of money would ever make me happy."

I could have written this about myself a few years ago. But when I took action by leaving a situation that, although financially rewarding, was no longer aligned with my personal mission, new doors of opportunity opened for me. It turned out to be the best decision of my professional life. Can you think of a time in your life when you made a difficult decision . . . but knew it was the right one even when others questioned you?

That was during the late fall of 1923. I found myself stranded in Columbus, Ohio, without funds, and worse still, without a plan by which to work my way out of my difficulty. It was the first time in my life that I had actually been stranded because of lack of funds.

Many times previously I had found money to be rather shy, but never before had I failed to get what I needed for my personal conveniences. The experience stunned me. I seemed totally at sea as to what I could or should do.

I thought of a dozen plans by which I might solve my problem, but dismissed them all as being either impractical or impossible of achievement. I felt like one who was lost in a jungle without a compass. Every attempt I made to work my way out brought me back to the original starting point.

For nearly two months I suffered with the worst of all human ailments: indecision. I knew the seventeen principles of personal achievement, but what I did not know was how to apply them! Without knowing it I was facing one of those emergencies of life through which, Mr. Carnegie had told me, men sometimes discover their "other selves."

My distress was so great that it never occurred to me to sit down and analyze its cause and seek its cure.

"The worst of all human ailments: indecision."

Have you ever felt paralyzed by indecision? This was the first major turning point in Napoleon Hill's life. His moving from job to job, seeking contentment and his own ideal professional life, sounds like many people today . . . people who are seeking contentment in their jobs and lives. Hill's predicament was, by his own admission, self-inflicted. However, he found himself in very much the same circumstances as someone today who has been negatively affected by the present economic situation. Hill took advantage of his temporary defeat, using it as a spur to force himself into thought and analysis—to find his "other self." If you have been dealt a blow by economic circumstances, you too can use it as a lever and motivation to find your "other self."

Defeat Is Converted into Victory

One afternoon I reached a decision through which I found the way out of my difficulty. I had a feeling that I wanted to get out into the "open spaces" of the country, where I could get a breath of fresh air and think.

I began to walk, and had gone seven or eight miles when I felt myself brought suddenly to a standstill. For several minutes I stood there as if I had been glued to my tracks. Everything around me went dark. I could hear the loud sound of some form of energy which was vibrating at a very high rate.

Then my nerves became quiet, my muscles relaxed, and a great calmness came over me. The atmosphere began to clear, and as it did so, I received a command from within which came in the form of a thought, as near as I can describe it.

The command was so clear and distinct that I could not misunderstand it. In substance it said, "The time has come for you to complete the philosophy of achievement which you began at Carnegie's suggestion. Go back home at once and begin transferring the data you have gathered from your own mind to written manuscripts." My "other self" had awakened.

For a few minutes I was frightened. The experience was unlike any I had ever undergone before. I turned and walked rapidly until I reached home. As I approached the house, I saw my three little boys looking out of a window of our house at our neighbor's children, who were dressing a Christmas tree in the house next door.

Then I recalled that it was Christmas Eve. Moreover, I recalled, with a feeling of deep distress such as I had never known before, that there would be no Christmas tree at our house. The look of disappointment on the faces of my children reminded me painfully of that fact.

I went into the house, sat down at my typewriter, and began at once to reduce to writing the discoveries I had made concerning the causes of success and failure. As I placed the first sheet of paper in the typewriter I was interrupted by that same strange feeling which had come over me out in the country a few hours before, and this thought flashed into my mind:

"Your mission in life is to complete the world's first philosophy of individual achievement. You have been trying in vain to escape your task, each effort having brought you failure. You are seeking happiness. Learn this lesson, once and forever, that you will find happiness only by helping others to find it! You have been a stubborn student. You had to be cured of your stubbornness through disappointment. Within a few years from now the whole world will start through an experience which will place millions of people in need of the philosophy which you have been directed to complete. Your big opportunity to find happiness by rendering useful service will have come. Go to work, and do not stop until you have completed and published the manuscripts which you have begun."

I was conscious of having arrived, at last, at the end of life's rainbow, and I was happy!

Doubt Makes Its Appearance

The "spell," if the experience may be so called, passed away. I began to write. Shortly thereafter my "reason" suggested to me that I was embarking upon a fool's mission. The idea of a man who was down and almost out presuming to write a philosophy of personal achievement seemed so ludicrous that I laughed hilariously, perhaps scornfully.

I squirmed in my chair, ran my fingers through my hair, and tried to create an alibi that would justify me in my own mind in taking the sheet of paper out of my typewriter before I had really begun to write, but the urge to continue was stronger than the desire to quit. I became reconciled to my task and went ahead.

"The urge to continue was stronger than the desire to quit."

Remember that time when you wanted to quit, but something drove you to keep going? It may have been your "other self."

Looking backward now, in the light of all that has happened, I can see that those minor experiences of adversity through which I had passed were among the most fortunate and profitable of all of my experiences. They were blessings in disguise because they forced me to continue a work which finally brought me an opportunity to make myself more useful to the world than I might have been had I succeeded in any previous plan or purpose.

For almost three months I worked on those manuscripts, completing them during the early part of 1924. As soon as they had been completed, I felt myself again being lured by the desire to get back into the great American game of business.

Succumbing to the lure, I purchased the Metropolitan Business College in Cleveland, Ohio, and began to lay plans for increasing its capacity. By the end of 1924 we had developed and expanded, by adding new courses, until we were doing a business nearly double the best previous record the school had ever known.

Again the germ of discontentment began to make itself felt in my blood. Again I knew that I could not find happiness in that sort of endeavor. I turned the business over to my associates and went on the lecture platform, lecturing on the philosophy of achievement, to the organization of which I had devoted so many of my previous years.

One night I was booked to lecture in Canton, Ohio. Fate, or whatever it is that seems sometimes to shape the destiny of men, no matter how hard they may try to battle against it, again stepped into the picture and brought me face to face with a painful experience.

In my Canton audience sat Don R. Mellett, publisher of the Canton *Daily News*. Mr. Mellett became so thoroughly interested in the philosophy of individual achievement on which I lectured that night that he invited me to come to see him the following day.

That visit resulted in a partnership agreement which was to have taken place on the first of the following January when Mr. Mellett planned to resign as publisher of the *Daily News*, to take charge of the business and publishing of the philosophy on which I had been working.

However, in July 1926, Mr. Mellett was murdered by Pat McDermott, an underworld character, and a Canton, Ohio, policeman, both of whom were sentenced to life imprisonment. He was murdered because he was exposing in his newspaper a hook-up between the bootleggers and certain members of the Canton police force. The crime was one of the most shocking that the prohibition era produced.

The July 1926 murder of crusading journalist Donald Ring Mellett, the editor of the Canton, Ohio, *Daily News*, was one of the most publicized crimes in the 1920s. In 1925 Mellett had discovered widespread corruption within the Canton police force and embarked on an anti-vice, anti-corruption editorial campaign, targeting, among others, the Canton police chief. Hill was reported to have asked Ohio's governor to initiate an investigation of the corruption, a detail not reflected in Hill's account.

Local underworld figures and at least one Canton police officer hired Patrick McDermott, an ex-con from Pennsylvania, to silence Mellett. Mellett was gunned down outside his home. As the story goes, gunmen were also lying in wait for Hill, but a fortuitous automotive breakdown kept him out of their way. On July 17, the *New York Times* reported in an article titled "More Death Threats Follow the Slaying of Canton Editor" that the citizens of Canton "are terror-stricken by threats of further killings by the rulers of the gamblers, bootleggers and other criminals." As recounted by Hill, after hearing of Mellett's murder and receiving an anonymous warning to get out of town, he fled to West Virginia. In large part due to the work of a private detective hired by the Stark County prosecutor, McDermott, two local gangsters, and a former police detective were ultimately convicted of Mellett's murder.

Chance (?) Saves My Life

The morning after Mr. Mellett's death I was called on the telephone and put on notice, by some unknown person, that I had one hour in which to get out of Canton; that I could go voluntarily within the hour, but if I waited longer I probably would go in a pine box. My business association with Mr. Mellett had apparently been misunderstood. His murderers evidently believed I was directly connected with the exposé he was making in his newspapers.

I did not wait for the one hour time limit to expire, but immediately got into my automobile and drove down to the home of relatives in the mountains of West Virginia, where I remained until the murderers had been placed in jail.

That experience came well within the category described by Mr. Carnegie as an "emergency" that forces men to think. For the first time in my life I knew the pain of constant fear. My experience of a few years before, in Columbus, had filled my mind with doubt and temporary indecision, but this one had filled it with a fear which I seemed unable to remove. During the time that I was in hiding I seldom left the house at night, and when I did step out I kept my hand on an automatic pistol in my coat pocket, with the safety catch unlatched for immediate action. If a strange automobile stopped in front of the house where I was hiding, I went into the basement and carefully scrutinized its occupants through the basement windows.

After some months of this sort of experience, my nerves began to crack. My courage had completely left me. The ambition which had heartened me during the long years of labor in my search for the causes of failure and success also had departed.

Slowly, step by step, I felt myself slipping into a state of lethargy from which I was afraid I should never be able to emerge. The feeling must have been closely akin to that experienced by one who suddenly steps into quicksand and realizes that every effort to extricate himself carries him just so much deeper. Fear is a self-generating morass.

If the seed of insanity had been in my make-up, surely it would have germinated during those months of living death. Foolish indecision, irresolute dreams, doubt and fear were my mind's concern, day and night.

The "emergency" I faced was disastrous in two ways. First, the very nature of it kept me in a constant state of indecision and fear. Secondly, the forced concealment kept me in idleness, with its attendant heaviness of time, which I naturally devoted to worry.

My reasoning faculty had almost been paralyzed. I realized that I had to work myself out of this state of mind. But how? The resourcefulness which had helped me to meet all previous emergencies seemed to have completely taken wing, leaving me helpless.

Out of my difficulties, which were burdensome enough up to this point, grew another which seemed more painful than all the others combined. It was the realization that I had spent the better portion of my past years in chasing a rainbow, searching hither and yon for the causes of success, and finding myself now more helpless than any of the 25,000 people whom I had judged as being "failures."

This thought was almost maddening. Moreover, it was extremely humiliating, because I had been lecturing all over the country, in schools and colleges and before business organizations, presuming to tell other people how to apply the seventeen principles of success, while here I was, unable to apply them myself. I was sure that I never could again face the world with a feeling of confidence.

Every time I looked at myself in a mirror I noticed an expression of self-contempt on my face, and not infrequently I did say things to the man in the mirror which are not printable. I had begun to place myself in the category of charlatans who offer others a remedy for failure which they themselves cannot successfully apply.

The criminals who had murdered Mr. Mellett had been tried and sent to the penitentiary for life; therefore, it was perfectly safe, as far as they were concerned, for me to come out of hiding and again take up my work. I could not come out, however, because now I faced circumstances more frightful than the criminals who had sent me into hiding.

The experience had destroyed whatever initiative I had possessed. I felt myself in the clutches of some depressing influence which seemed like a nightmare. I was alive; I could move around, but I could not think of a single move by which I might continue to seek the goal which I had, at Mr. Carnegie's suggestion, set for myself. I was rapidly becoming indifferent, not only toward myself, but worse still, I was becoming grouchy and irritable toward those who had given me shelter during my "emergency."

I faced the greatest emergency of my life. Unless you have gone through a similar experience, you cannot possibly know how I felt. Such experiences cannot be described. To be understood they must be felt.

"My reasoning faculty had almost been paralyzed."

Hill was paralyzed first by fear of physical harm and then by the shame of having been paralyzed by that fear. Have you ever been paralyzed by similar emotions? When you are faced with your own "emergency," fear can either motivate you or paralyze you. By recognizing that you have a choice and reacting positively to your fears, you can permanently change your life for the better. Many people today may be experiencing the same feelings of anger followed by irritability and the debilitating feeling of indifference. They feel discouraged and lack self-confidence due to uncertainty in their financial situation or personal lives. They may be angry and allow that anger to paralyze them. I had a conversation with just such a young man. "I am 30 years old," he said, "and have no marketable skills or prospects." He had a million excuses for not taking action to change his situation. I pointed out that unless he took action nothing would change. "Unless you make an effort to change things," I said, "in a year's time the only difference will be that you are 31 years old with no marketable skills or prospects." Does this pattern sound familiar to you, either for yourself or someone you care for? How do you break that paralysis? Napoleon Hill now shares how he overcame his fear and indifference and found the hope, inspiration, and motivation to recover and create success in his life.

The Most Dramatic Moment of My Life

The turn came suddenly, in fall 1927, more than a year after the Canton incident. I left the house one night and walked up to the public school building, on top of a hill above the town.

I had reached a decision to fight the matter out with myself before that night ended. I began to walk around the building, trying to force my befuddled brain to think clearly. I must have made several hundred trips around the building before anything which even remotely resembled organized thought began to take place in my mind. As I walked I repeated over and over to myself, "There is a way out and I am going to find it before I go back to the house." I must have repeated that sentence a thousand times. Moreover, I meant exactly what I was saying. I was thoroughly disgusted with myself, but I entertained a hope of salvation.

Then like a flash of lightning out of a clear sky, an idea burst into my mind with such force that the impulse drove my blood up and down my veins:

"This is your testing time. You have been reduced to poverty and humiliated in order that you might be forced to discover your 'other self.'"

If today's economic times have dealt you a blow, moving you toward poverty, embarrassing you, or damaging your self-confidence, consider it a test, just as Napoleon Hill did in the late 1920s and early 1930s. Force yourself to discover your "other self." By working through the low points in your life and persevering, you can gain the insight needed to succeed.

For the first time in years I recalled what Mr. Carnegie had said about this "other self." I recalled now that he said I would discover it toward the end of my labor of research into the causes of failure and success, and that the discovery usually came as the result of an emergency, when men are forced to change their habits and to think their way out of difficulty.

I continued to walk around the school house, but now I was walking on air. Subconsciously I seemed to know that I was about to be released from the self-made prison into which I had cast myself.

I realized that this great emergency had brought me an opportunity, not merely to discover my "other self," but to test the soundness of the philosophy of achievement which I had been teaching others as being workable. Soon I would know whether it would work or not. I made up my mind that if it did not work I would burn the manuscripts I had written and never again be guilty of telling other people that they were "the masters of their fate, the captains of their souls."

Hill is paraphrasing from the poem "Invictus," published in 1888 by William Ernest Henley (1849–1903).

Out of the night that covers me,
Black as the Pit from pole to pole,
I thank whatever gods may be
For my unconquerable soul.

In the fell clutch of circumstance
I have not winced nor cried aloud.
Under the bludgeonings of chance
My head is bloody, but unbowed.

Beyond this place of wrath and tears
Looms but the Horror of the shade,
And yet the menace of the years
Finds, and shall find, me unafraid.

It matters not how strait the gate,
How charged with punishments the scroll.
I am the master of my fate:
I am the captain of my soul.

The full moon was just rising over the mountain top. I had never seen it shine so brightly before. As I stood gazing at it, another thought flashed into my mind. It was this:

"You have been telling other people how to master fear and how to surmount the difficulties which arise out of the emergencies of life. From now on you can speak with authority because you are about to rise above your own difficulties with courage and purpose, resolute and unafraid."

With that thought came a change in the chemistry of my being which lifted me into a state of exultation I had never before known. My brain began to clear itself of the state of lethargy into which it had lapsed. My faculty of reason began to work once more.

For a brief moment I was happy to have had the privilege of going through those long months of torment, because the experience provided an opportunity for me to test the soundness of the principles of achievement which I had so laboriously wrested from my research.

When this thought came to me, I stopped still, drew my feet closely together, saluted (I did not know what or whom), and stood rigidly at attention for several minutes. This seemed, at first, like a foolish thing to do, but while I was standing there another thought came through in the form of an "order" that was as brief and snappy as any ever given by a military commander to a subordinate.

The order said, "Tomorrow get into your automobile and drive to Philadelphia, where you will receive aid in publishing your philosophy of achievement."

There was no further explanation and no modification of the order. As soon as I received it, I walked back to the house, went to bed, and slept with peace of mind such as I had not known for over a year.

When I awoke the following morning, I got out of bed and immediately began to pack my clothes and make ready for the trip to Philadelphia. My reason told me that I was embarking upon a fool's mission. Who did I know in Philadelphia to whom I might apply for financial aid in publishing eight volumes of books at a cost of $25,000? I asked myself.

Instantly the answer to that question flashed into my mind, as plainly as if it had been uttered in audible words: "You are following orders now, instead of asking questions. Your 'other self' will be in charge during this trip."

There was another condition which seemed to make my preparation to go to Philadelphia absurd. I had no money!

This thought had barely occurred to me when my "other self" exploded it by giving another sharp order, saying, "Ask your brother-in-law for fifty dollars and he will lend it to you."

The order seemed definite and final. Without further hesitation I followed instructions. When I asked my brother-in-law for the money, he said, "Why, certainly you can have fifty dollars, but if you are going to be gone very long you had better take a hundred dollars." I thanked him and said I thought fifty dollars would be enough. I knew it was not enough, but that was the amount my "other self" had commanded me to ask for and that is the amount I secured.

I was greatly relieved when I found that my brother-in-law was not going to ask me why I was going to Philadelphia. If he had known all that had taken place in my mind during the previous night, he perhaps would have thought I should go to a psychiatric hospital for treatment instead of going to Philadelphia on a wild-goose chase.

My "Other Self" Takes Command

I left with my head telling me I was a fool and my "other self" commanding me to ignore the challenge and carry out my instructions.

I drove all night, arriving in Philadelphia the next morning. My first thought was to look up a modestly priced boarding house where I could rent a room for about one dollar a day.

Here again my "other self" took charge and gave the command to register at the most exclusive hotel in the city. With a little more than forty dollars of my remaining capital in my pocket, it seemed like financial suicide when I marched up to the desk and asked for a room; or rather I should say I started to ask for a room when my newly discovered "other self" gave the order to ask for a suite of rooms, the cost of which would about consume my remaining capital in two days. I obeyed.

The bell-boy picked up my bags, handed me my claim check for my automobile, and bowed me toward the elevator as if I were the Prince of Wales. It was the first time in more than a year that any human being had shown me such deference. My own relatives, with whom I had been living, far from having shown me deference, had (so I imagined) felt I was a burden on their hands, and I am sure that I was, because no man in the frame of mind that I had been in for the past year could be anything other than a burden to all with whom he came into contact.

It was becoming apparent that my "other self" was determined to wean me away from the inferiority complex which I had developed.

I tossed the bell-boy a dollar. I started to estimate what my hotel bill would be by the end of the week when my "other self" commanded me to get my mind entirely off of all thoughts of limitation, and to conduct myself, for the time being, just as I would if I had all the money I wanted in my pockets.

The experience I was passing through was both new and strange to me. I had never posed as being anything other than what I believed myself to be.

For nearly half an hour this "other self" gave orders which I followed to the letter during the subsequent period of my stay in Philadelphia. The instructions were given through the medium of thoughts which presented themselves in my mind with such force that they were readily distinguishable from my ordinary self-created thoughts.

Hill took on the persona of the wealthy man he wanted to be. We strongly agree that to be wealthy you need to think wealthy. It is also important to be in the right environment. Don Green, CEO of the Napoleon Hill Foundation, once told me, "I first bought my good suits from Sobel's, a custom clothing store—where Eastman Kodak executives shopped. The owner had a sign behind the register that said, "If you want to be a success, you must first dress the part."

However, we recommend moderation in trying to emulate Mr. Hill in spending money that he did not have.

I Receive Strange "Orders" from a Strange Source

My instructions began in this fashion:

"You are now completely in charge of your 'other self.' You are entitled to know that two entities occupy your body, as in fact two similar entities occupy the body of each living person on earth.

"One of these entities is motivated by and responds to the impulse of fear. The other is motivated by and responds to the impulse of faith. For more than a year you have been driven, like a slave, by the fear entity.

"Night before last the faith entity gained control over your physical body, and you are now motivated by that entity. For the sake of convenience you may call this faith entity your 'other self.' It knows no limitations, has no fears, and recognizes no such word as 'impossible.'

"You were directed to select this environment of luxury, in a good hotel, as a means of discouraging the return to power of the fear entity. That fear-motivated 'old self' is not dead; it has merely been dethroned. And it will follow you around wherever you go, awaiting a favorable opportunity to step in and take charge of you again. It can gain control of you only through your thoughts. Remember this, and keep the doors to your mind tightly closed against all thoughts which seek to limit you in any manner whatsoever, and you will be safe.

"Do not permit yourself to worry about the money you will need for your immediate expenses. That will come to you by the time you must have it.

"Now, let us get down to business. First of all you should know that the faith entity now in charge of your body performs no miracles, nor does it work in opposition to any of nature's laws. As long as it is in charge of your body it will guide you when you call on it, through impulses of thought which it will place in your mind, in carrying out your plans through the most logical and convenient natural media available.

"Above everything else, get this fact clearly fixed in your mind, that your 'other self' will not do your work for you; it will only guide you intelligently in achieving for yourself the objects of your desires.

Will you be guided by faith?
Or will you allow fear to overtake you?

"This 'other self' will aid you in translating your plans into reality. Moreover, you should know that it begins, always, with your major, or most pronounced desire. At this time your major desire—the one which brought you here—is to publish and distribute the results of your research into the causes of success and failure. You estimate that you will need approximately $25,000.

"Among your acquaintances there is a man who will supply you with this needed capital. Begin, at once, to call into your mind the names of all persons of your acquaintance whom you have reason to believe might be induced to furnish the financial aid you require.

"When the name of the logical person comes into your mind, you will recognize it immediately. Communicate with that person and the aid you seek will be given. In your approach, however, present your request in terminology such as you would use in the usual course of business transactions. Make no reference whatsoever to this introduction you have had to your 'other self.' If you violate these instructions, you will meet with temporary defeat.

"Your 'other self' will remain in charge and continue to direct you as long as you rely upon it. Keep doubt and fear and worry, and all thoughts of limitation, entirely out of your mind.

"That will be all for the present. You will now begin to move of your own free will, precisely as you did before you discovered your 'other self.' Physically you are the same as you have always been; therefore, no one will recognize that any change has taken place in you."

I looked around the room, blinked my eyes, and to make sure that I was not dreaming, I got up and walked over to a mirror and looked at myself closely. The expression on my face had changed from one of doubt to one of courage and faith.

There was no longer any doubt in my mind that my physical body was in charge of an influence far different from the one which had been dethroned two nights before, as I walked around that school house in West Virginia.

Here, in editing the manuscript, I have ended the chapter at one of the great turning points in the author's life. Have you ever undergone a life change such as the one Hill describes above? It can also be described, in religious terms, as a conversion experience. Others may simply refer to it as "a wake-up call" or "a tap on the shoulder" or more vehemently as "a slap in the face!"

✦ *Chapter Two* ✦

A NEW WORLD IS REVEALED TO ME

OBVIOUSLY I HAD UNDERGONE A NEW BIRTH by which I had been separated from all forms of fear. I now had courage such as I never before had experienced. Despite the fact that I had not as yet been shown how, or from what source, I would be able to secure the necessary funds which I was seeking, I had such absolute faith that the money would be forthcoming that I could see it already in my possession.

On but few occasions in my entire life have I experienced such faith. It was a feeling which one person cannot describe to another. There are no words in the English language suitable for such a description—a fact that all who have had similar experiences can easily verify.

I proceeded immediately to carry out the instructions I had received. All feeling that I had embarked upon an impossible mission had now left me. One by one I began to call into my mind the names of all my acquaintances I knew to be financially able to supply me with the $25,000 which I needed, starting with the name of Henry Ford, and going over the entire list of more than three hundred people. My "other self" plainly said, "Keep on searching."

The Darkest Hour Is Just Before Dawn

But I had come to the end of my rope. My entire list of acquaintances had been exhausted, and with it my physical endurance as well. I had been at work, concentrating my mind upon that list of names, for the better part of two days and nights, having stopped only long enough to sleep for a few hours.

I leaned back in my chair, shut my eyes, and went into a sort of doze for a few minutes. I was aroused by what seemed to be an explosion in the room. As I regained consciousness the name of Albert L. Pelton came into my mind . . . and with it a plan which I knew instantly to be the plan through which I would succeed in getting Mr. Pelton to publish my books. I remembered Mr. Pelton only as an advertiser in *The Golden Rule* magazine, which I had formerly published.

Hill's subconscious mind identified an acquaintance, remembered only as an advertiser in Hill's magazine, as a potential source of funding. You make an impression on everyone you meet, just as everyone you meet makes an impression on you. You never know when an acquaintance may become a business associate. There is great power in your network.

I sent for a typewriter, addressed a letter to Mr. Pelton at Meriden, Connecticut, and described the plan just as it had been handed over to me. He answered by telegram, saying that he would be in Philadelphia to see me the following day.

When he came I showed him the original manuscripts of my philosophy, and briefly explained what I believed its mission to be. He turned through the pages of the manuscripts for a few minutes, then stopped suddenly and fixed his eyes on the wall for a few seconds and said, "I will publish your books for you."

The contract was drawn; a substantial advance payment on royalties was given me, the manuscripts were turned over to him, and he took them back to Meriden.

I did not ask him at the time what caused him to reach a decision to publish my books before he had read the manuscripts, but I do know that he supplied the necessary capital, printed the books, and assisted me in selling many thousands of sets of them to his own clientele of book buyers, who were located in practically every English-speaking country in the world.

My "Other Self" Makes Good

Three months from the day that Mr. Pelton called on me in Philadelphia, a completed set of my books was placed on the table in front of me, and my income from the sale of the books began to run high enough for all my needs. These books are now in the hands of my students all over the world.

My first royalty check from the sale of my books was for $850. As I opened the envelope in which it came, my "other self" said, "Your only limitation is the one which you set up in your own mind!"

"Your only limitation is the one which you set up in your own mind!"

Does this statement ring as true for you as it does for me? So many times I have been my own worst enemy and needlessly held myself back through a lack of self-confidence. Hill wants us all to discover our "other self" so we can each reach our maximum potential.

I am not sure that I understand just what this "other self" is, but I do know that there can be no permanent defeat for the man or the woman who discovers it and relies upon it.

The day after Mr. Pelton came to see me in Philadelphia, my "other self" presented me with an idea which solved my immediate financial problem. The idea flashed into my mind that automobile merchandising methods had to undergo a drastic change and that future salesmen in this field would have to learn to sell automobiles instead of merely serving as buyers of used car trade-ins, as most of them were doing at the time.

It also occurred to me that young men who had just finished college and who, therefore, knew nothing of the old "tricks" of automobile merchandising would be the material out of which this new brand of salesmen could best be developed.

The idea was so distinct and impressive that I immediately called the sales manager of the General Motors Company on long-distance telephone and briefly explained my plan to him. He too was impressed by it and referred me to the West Philadelphia branch of the Buick Automobile Company, which was then owned and managed by Earl Powell. I went to see Mr. Powell, explained my plan to him, and he retained me at once to train fifteen carefully selected young college men through whom the plan was put into operation.

My income from that retainer was more than enough to take care of all of my expenses for the following three months, until the returns from the sale of my books began to come in, including the cost of that expensive suite of rooms, over which I had at first been so concerned.

My "other self" had not disappointed me. The money I needed was in my hands at the proper time, just as I had been assured the money would be. By this time I had been convinced that my trip to Philadelphia was by no means a fool's mission, as my reason had indicated it would be before I left West Virginia.

From that time right up to this very minute everything I have needed has come to me, and this despite the fact that the whole world has recently passed through a period of economic depression, when the bare necessities of life have not always been available to all people. Sometimes the arrival of the material things I needed has been a little late, but I can truthfully say that my "other self" has always met me at the cross-roads when I have come to them, and indicated which path I should follow.

The "other self" follows no precedents, recognizes no limitations, and always finds a way to accomplish desired ends! It may meet with temporary defeat, but not with permanent failure. I am as sure of the soundness of this statement as I am of the fact of being engaged in writing these lines.

The "other self" may "meet with temporary defeat, but not with permanent failure." How many times do we allow a temporary defeat to affect us as if it were a permanent failure instead of learning from it and moving on? As Hill describes, he himself faced many setbacks along his journey, but each time he was able to find the seed of greater benefit and move on to greater successes.

Meanwhile, I earnestly hope that some of the millions of men and women who have been wounded by the business depression and other unpleasant experiences will discover within themselves this strange entity which I have called my "other self," and that the discovery will lead them, as it has led me, into a closer relationship with that source of power which surmounts obstacles and masters difficulties, instead of being mastered by them. There is a great power to be discovered in your "other self"! Search sincerely and you will find it.

Hill's work was published during the Great Depression and indeed helped millions of people find hope and courage to live in faith that they would find their own paths to success. I believe we can find many parallels between his time and our own. It is during periods of great stress that we find our will and our inner strength. With the current economic uncertainties, people are choosing—or being forced—to find new paths to provide for themselves and their families, and many will find great success. They will be the great stories of success we will be reading about a few years from now. Will you be among those success stories or still watching from the sidelines?

"Failure": A Blessing in Disguise

I have made another discovery as the result of this introduction to my "other self," namely, that there is a solution for every legitimate problem, no matter how difficult the problem may seem.

"There is a solution for every legitimate problem, no matter how difficult the problem may seem."

While this concept may be difficult to acknowledge when you are in the midst of the storm, hindsight generally proves it true.

I have also discovered that there comes with every experience of temporary defeat, and every failure and every form of adversity, the seed of an equivalent benefit.

Mind you, I did not say the full-blown flower of success, but the seed from which that flower may be made to germinate and grow. I know of no exception to this rule. The seed of which I speak may not always be observed, but you may be sure it is there, in one form or another.

I do not pretend to understand all about this strange force which reduced me to poverty and want, and filled me with fear, and then gave me a new birth of faith through which I have been privileged to extend help to tens of thousands who found themselves slipping. But I do know that such a force has come into my life and that I am doing all I can to place others in communication with it.

During my quarter-century of research into the causes of success and failure I have discovered many principles of truth which have been helpful to me and to others, but nothing I have observed has impressed me more than the discovery that every great leader of the past, whose record I have examined, was beset by difficulties and met with temporary defeat before "arriving."

"Every great leader of the past, whose record I have examined, was beset by difficulties and met with temporary defeat before 'arriving.'"

Failure and temporary defeat are part of the journey to finding true success.

From Christ on down to Edison, the men who have achieved most have been those who met with the most stubborn forms of temporary defeat. This would seem to justify the conclusion that Infinite Intelligence has a plan, or a law, by which it hurdles men over many obstacles before giving them the privilege of leadership or the opportunity to render useful service in a noteworthy fashion.

I would not wish to be again subjected to the experiences through which I passed during that fateful Christmas Eve in 1923, and since, on that eventful evening when I walked around the school house in West Virginia and fought that terrible battle with fear, but all the wealth in the world would not induce me to divest myself of the knowledge I have gained from those experiences.

Faith Has a New Meaning to Me

I repeat that I do not know exactly what this "other self" is, but I know enough about it to lean upon it in a spirit of absolute faith in times of difficulty, when the ordinary reasoning faculty of my mind seems to be inadequate for my needs.

The economic depression which started in 1929 brought misery to millions of people, but let us not forget that the experience also brought many blessings, not the least of these being the knowledge that there is something infinitely worse than being forced to work. It is being forced not to work. In the main, that depression was more of a blessing than it was a curse, if analyzed in the light of the changes it brought to the minds of those who were wounded by it. The same is true of every experience which changes men's habits and forces them to turn to the great "within" for the solution of their problems.

"There is something infinitely worse than being forced to work. It is being forced not to work. In the main, that depression was more of a blessing than it was a curse, if analyzed in the light of the changes it brought."

Is Hill being harsh here, or is he looking beyond the immediate cause and effect of economic disaster to the underlying spiritual result that comes from a true crisis? Can our present economic travails be more of a blessing than a curse? Can economic hardship, such as the loss of a job, be a blessing in disguise? Perhaps yes, if the result is the awakening of an entrepreneurial spirit and the creation of a new business.

The time which I spent in seclusion in West Virginia was, by great odds, the most severe punishment of my life, but the experience brought blessings in the form of needed knowledge which more than offset the suffering which it cost me. These two results—the suffering and the knowledge gained from it—were inevitable. The law of compensation, which Emerson so clearly defined, made this result both natural and necessary.

Ralph Waldo Emerson (1803–1882) explained the law of compensation in very clear terms: "For everything you have missed, you have gained something else; and for everything you gain, you lose something else." In his journal dated January 8, 1826, he also wrote, "The whole of what we know is a system of compensations. Every defect in one manner is made up in another. Every suffering is rewarded; every sacrifice is made up; every debt is paid."

What the future may hold for me in the way of disappointment, through temporary defeat, I of course have no way of knowing. I do know, however, that no experience of the future can possibly wound me as deeply as have some of those of the past, because I am now on speaking terms at least with my "other self."

Since this "other self" took charge of me, I have come by useful knowledge which I am sure I never would have discovered while my old fear entity was on the throne. For one thing I have learned that those who meet with difficulties which seem insurmountable may, if they will do so, best overcome these difficulties by forgetting them for a time and helping others who have greater problems.

The Value of Giving Before Trying to Get

I am sure that no effort which we extend to those who are in distress can go without some form of adequate reward. Not always does the reward come from those to whom the service is rendered, but it will come from one source or another.

I seriously doubt that any man can avail himself of the benefits of his "other self" as long as he is steeped in greed and avarice, envy and fear, but if I am wrong in this conclusion then I still have the unusual honor of being one who has found peace of mind and happiness through a viewpoint that was not sound. I would prefer being thus wrong and happy, to being right and unhappy! But this viewpoint is not wrong!

As long as I remain on good terms with my "other self" I shall be able to acquire every material thing that I need. Moreover, I shall be able to find happiness and peace of mind. What more could anyone else accomplish?

The sole motive which inspired me to write this book was a sincere desire to be helpful to others by sharing with them as much as they may be prepared to accept of the stupendous fortune which became mine the moment I discovered my "other self." This fortune, happily, is one that cannot be measured in material or financial terms alone, because it is greater than everything which such things represent.

Material and financial fortunes, when reduced to their most liquid terms, are measurable in terms of bank balances. Bank balances are no stronger than banks. This other fortune of which I speak is measurable, not only in terms of peace of mind and contentment but as manifested in those adept at prayer.

My "other self" has taught me to concentrate upon my purpose and to forget about the plan by which it is to be attained when I go to prayer. I am not suggesting that material objects may be acquired without plans. What I am saying is that the power which translates one's thoughts or desires into realities has its source in an Infinite Intelligence which knows more about plans than the one doing the praying.

Stating the case in another way, may it not be wise, when praying, to trust to the Universal Mind to hand over the plan best suited for the attainment of the object of that prayer? My experience with prayer has taught me that so often all which results from prayer is a plan (if the prayer is answered at all), a plan that is suited for the attainment of the object of the prayer through natural and material media. The plan must be transmuted, through self-effort action.

I know nothing about any form of prayer which can be induced to work favorably in a mind that is colored, in the slightest degree, by fear.

Is prayer a part of your life? Do you trust God to "hand over the plan best suited for the attainment of the object" of your prayer? Do you acknowledge that in order for your plan to be successful you must take action?

A New Way to Pray

Since becoming better acquainted with my "other self," my way of praying is different from what it was before. I used to go to prayer only when facing difficulty. Now I go to prayer before difficulty overtakes me, when possible. I now pray, not for more of this world's goods and greater blessings, but to be worthy of that which I already have. I find that this plan is better than the old one.

Infinite Intelligence seems not at all offended when I give thanks and show that I am grateful for the blessings which have crowned my efforts. I was astounded, when I first tried this plan of offering a prayer of thanks for what I already possessed, to discover what a vast fortune I had owned without being appreciative of it.

For example, I discovered that I possessed a sound body which had never been seriously damaged by illness. I had a mind which was reasonably well balanced. I had a creative imagination through which I could render useful service to great numbers of people. I was blessed with all the freedom I desired, in both body and mind. I possessed an imperishable desire to help others who were less fortunate.

I discovered that happiness, the highest aim of mankind, was mine for the taking, business depression or no business depression.

Last, but by no means least, I discovered that I had the privilege of approaching Infinite Intelligence, either for the purpose of offering thanks for what I already possessed, or to ask for more, and for guidance.

It may be helpful for every reader of this book to take inventory of his or her intangible assets. Such an inventory may disclose possessions of priceless value.

May we all make an inventory of our blessings in life. And give thanks for every gift that we have been given. I know that when I am at a low point in my life, I force myself to think of my family and friends and the blessings they have brought to my life. It is the quickest path up and puts my temporary setbacks into perspective.

Some Signs We Have Overlooked

The whole world is undergoing a change of such stupendous proportions that millions of people have become panic-stricken with worry, doubt, indecision, and fear! It seems to me that now is a splendid time for those who have come to the cross-roads of doubt to endeavor to become acquainted with their "other selves."

All who wish to do so will find it helpful if they take a lesson from nature. Observation will show that the eternal stars shine nightly in their accustomed places; that the sun continues to send down its rays of warmth, causing Mother Earth to yield an over-abundance of food and clothing; that water continues to flow down hill; that the birds of the air and the wild animals of the forest receive their accustomed requirements of food; that useful day follows restful night; that busy summer follows the inactive winter; that the seasons come and go precisely as they did before the 1929 depression began; that, in reality, only men's minds have ceased to function normally, and this, because men have filled their minds with fear. Observation of these simple facts of everyday life may be helpful as a starting point for those who wish to supplant fear by faith.

I am not a prophet, but I can, with all due modesty, predict that every individual has the power to change his or her material or financial status by first changing the nature of his or her beliefs.

"Every individual has the power to change his or her material or financial status by first changing the nature of his or her beliefs."

It was right after publication of *Think and Grow Rich* in 1937 that Napoleon Hill began this manuscript for *Outwitting the Devil*. Through his interview with the Devil, Hill discovers and reveals how the Devil may be "having his way" with you and how you can ignite your "other self" to not only conquer the Devil in your own life but to also empower your "other self" to achieve your greatest success! Throughout his work is the recurring theme of the importance of transforming your thoughts from fear to faith.

Do not confuse the word "belief" with the word "wish." The two are not the same. Everyone is capable of "wishing" for financial, material, or spiritual advantages, but the element of faith is the only sure power by which a wish may be translated into a belief, and a belief into reality.

And right here is an appropriate place at which to call attention to a real benefit which anyone may experience by deliberately using faith in focusing attention upon any form of constructive desire. The mind acts upon one's dominating, or most pronounced desires. There is no escape from this fact. It is a fact indeed. "Be careful what you set your heart upon, for it surely shall be yours."

Faith Is the Beginning of All Great Achievement

If Edison had stopped by merely wishing for the secret with which electric energy might be harnessed and made to serve through the incandescent lamp, that convenience to civilization would have remained among nature's multifarious secrets. He met with temporary defeat more than 10,000 times before wresting this secret from nature. It was finally yielded up to him because he believed it would be, and he kept on trying until he had the answer.

Edison uncovered more of nature's secrets (they might have been called "miracles" at an earlier period) in the realm of physics than did any other man who ever lived, and this because he became acquainted with his "other self." I have his own word for this, but even if I did not have it, his achievements of themselves have disclosed the secret in their unfoldment.

Nothing within reason is impossible to the man who knows and relies upon his "other self." Whatever man believes to be true has a way of becoming true.

A prayer is a released thought, sometimes expressed in audible words and at other times expressed silently. I have observed by experience that a silent prayer is as efficacious as the one which is expressed in words. I have observed also that one's state of mind is the determining factor when prayer works, as well as when it does not.

My conception of the "other self" which I have tried to describe is that it merely symbolizes a newly discovered approach to Infinite Intelligence, an approach which one may control and direct through the simple process of mixing faith with one's thoughts. This is only another way of saying that I now have greater faith in the power of prayer.

The state of mind known as faith apparently opens to one the medium of a sixth sense through which one may communicate with sources of power and information far surpassing any available through the five physical senses. There comes to your aid, and to do your bidding, with the development of the sixth sense, a strange power which, let us assume, is a guardian angel who can open to you at all times the door to the Temple of Wisdom. The "sixth sense" comes as near to being a miracle as anything I have ever experienced, and it appears so perhaps because I do not understand the method by which this principle is operated.

This much I do know—that there is a power or a first cause, or an Intelligence which permeates every atom of matter, and embraces every unit of energy perceptible to man; that this Infinite Intelligence converts acorns into oak trees, causes water to flow downhill in response to the law of gravity, follows night with day, and winter with summer, each maintaining its proper place and relationship to the other. This Intelligence may aid in transmuting one's desires into concrete or material form. I have this knowledge because I have experimented with it and have experienced it.

I have for many years followed the habit of taking personal inventory of myself once a year, for the purpose of determining how many of my weaknesses I have bridged or eliminated, and to ascertain what progress, if any, I had made during the year.

This section on faith is worth rereading a few times because it contains Hill's core teachings on prayer. Faith, in his view, is a "sixth sense" or spiritual power that enables one to succeed if one is in step with the first cause of all things—one of his descriptions of God. His is a practical or "scientific" faith that emphasizes tangible results.

In the book *Three Feet from Gold* my co-author and I discuss the Personal Success Equation that clearly reveals the importance of faith:

((P + T) x A x A) + F = Your Personal Success Equation

Combining your Passion with your Talent and then seeking the right Association and taking the right Action are very important components for Success . . . but it is when you combine all those components with a strong Faith in yourself and your mission that you truly have Your Personal Success Equation.

✦ *Chapter Three* ✦

A STRANGE INTERVIEW WITH THE DEVIL

WHILE YOU ARE READING THE INTERVIEW with the Devil, you will recognize from the brief description I have given you of the history of my life what a desperate effort the Devil made to muzzle me before I gained public recognition. You will understand also, after reading the interview with the Devil, why the interview had to be preceded by this personal history of my background.

Before you begin to read the interview, I want you to have a clear picture of the final fling the Devil had at me, and be it remembered with profit that it was this final fling which gave mercy a chance to turn and twist the Devil's tail until he squealed out his confession.

The Devil's undoing began with the depression in 1929. Through that fortunate turn of the Wheel of Life, I lost my 600-acre estate in the Catskill Mountains; my income was entirely cut off; the Harriman National Bank, in which all my funds were deposited, folded up and was wiped out. Before I realized what was happening, I found myself caught up in a spiritual and economic hurricane which evolved into a worldwide catastrophe of such force that no individual or group of individuals could withstand it.

While waiting for the storm to cease and the stampede of human fear to stop, I moved to Washington, D.C., the city from which I made my start after my first meeting with Andrew Carnegie, nearly a quarter of a century previously.

There seemed nothing for me to do except sit down and wait. All I had was time. After three years of waiting without tangible results, my restless soul began to push me back into service.

There was little opportunity for me to teach a philosophy

of success when the world around me was in the midst of abject failure, and men's minds were filled with the fear of poverty.

This thought came to me one evening while I was sitting in my automobile, in front of the Lincoln Memorial on the Potomac River, within the shadow of the Capitol. With it came another thought: The world had staged an unprecedented depression over which no human being had control. With that depression had come to me an opportunity to test the philosophy of self-determination, to the organization of which I had devoted the better portion of my adult life. Once more I had the opportunity to learn whether my philosophy was practical or mere theory.

I realized too the opportunity had come to test a claim I had made hundreds of times that "every adversity brings with it the seed of an equivalent advantage." What, if any, I asked myself, were the advantages to me of a world depression?

When I began to look for a direction in which I might move to test my philosophy, I made the most shocking discovery of my life. I discovered that through some strange power which I did not understand, I had lost my courage; my initiative had been demoralized; my enthusiasm had been weakened. Worst of all, I was sorely ashamed to acknowledge that I was the author of a philosophy of self-determination, because down deep in my heart I knew, or thought I knew, that I could not make my philosophy pull me out of the hole of despair in which I found myself.

While I floundered in a state of mental bewilderment, the Devil must have been dancing a jig of rejoicing. At last he had "the author of the world's first philosophy of individual achievement" pinned under his thumb and paralyzed with indecision.

But the Devil's opposition must have been at work too!

✦ ✦ ✦ ✦ ✦ ✦ ✦ ✦ ✦ ✦

As I sat there in front of the Lincoln Memorial, reviewing in retrospect the circumstances which had so many times previously lifted me to great heights of achievement, only to let me drop to equal depths of despair, a happy thought was handed over to me in the form of a definite plan of action by which I believed I could throw off that hypnotic feeling of indifference with which I had been bound.

In the interview with the Devil, the exact nature of the power by which I had been deprived of my initiative and courage has been described. It is the same power with which millions of others were bound during the Great Depression. It is the chief weapon with which the Devil ensnares and controls human beings.

The sum and substance of this thought which came to me was this: Despite the fact that I had learned from Andrew Carnegie and more than five hundred others of equal business and professional achievements that noteworthy achievements in all walks of life come through the application of the Master Mind (the harmonious coordination of two or more minds working to a definite end), I had failed to make such an alliance for the purpose of carrying out my plan to take the philosophy of individual achievement to the world.

Despite the fact I had understood the power of the Master Mind, I had neglected to appropriate and use this power. I had been laboring as a "lone wolf" instead of allying myself with other and superior minds.

The interview with the Devil may have occurred as Hill sat at the foot of the Lincoln Memorial. Was it real? It was real to Hill and created the framework for how he lived his life and shared his revelations with us: his students. To reiterate Hill's earlier words, he had discovered that "every great leader of the past, whose record I have examined, was beset by difficulties and met with temporary defeat before 'arriving.'" Hill also describes in his works how these great leaders surrounded themselves with Master Minds. They conquered their inner struggles with adversity and then used the power of the Master Mind to propel their successes. Consider how you could form a Master Mind group—a team—to help you overcome adversity and propel you to success.

An Analysis

Let us now briefly analyze the strange interview you are about to begin. Some who read will want to ask, after they finish it, "Did you really interview the Devil, or did you merely interview an imaginary Devil?" Some may wish the answer to this question before they begin the interview.

I will answer in the only truthful way I could answer . . . by saying that the Devil I interviewed may have been real, just as he claimed to be, or he may have been the creation of my own imagination. Whichever he was, whether real or imaginary, is of little importance compared with the nature of the information conveyed through the interview.

The important question is this: Does the interview convey dependable information which may be helpful to people who are trying to find their places in the world? If it conveys that sort of information, no matter whether it is conveyed in the form of fact or fiction, then it is worthy of serious analysis through careful reading. I am not concerned in the least as to the real source of the information or as to the real nature of the Devil whose astounding story you are about to read. I am concerned only with the fact that the Devil's confession squares perfectly with what I have seen of life.

I believe the interview does convey information of practical benefit to all who have not found life to be friendly, and the reason I believe so is the fact that I have made the central theme of this book yield to me all the happiness I need, in the form best suited to my nature.

I have had experience with enough of the principles mentioned by the Devil to assure me that they will do exactly what he says they will. That is enough for me. So I pass the story of the interview on to you for whatever you may be able to make it pay in useful dividends.

Perhaps you will get the greatest values if you accept the Devil as being what he claims himself to be, relying upon his message for whatever it may bring you that you can use, and not worrying as to who the Devil is or whether he exists.

If you want my honest personal opinion, I believe the Devil is exactly who he claims to be. Now let us analyze his strange confession.

After forcing his way into the consciousness of the Devil, "Mr. Earthbound" began the unwilling interview with questions which could not be evaded . . .

Hill, "Mr. Earthbound," interrogates the Devil in an almost courtroom atmosphere. Somehow, the Devil is obligated to give complete and accurate answers. How was this done? Perhaps Hill forced the Devil's confession by forming a Master Mind, possibly with his wife, "the harmonious coordination of two or more minds working to a definite end" to exert the power of God—"the great storehouse of Infinite Intelligence wherein is stored all that is, all that ever was, and all that can ever be." Perhaps Hill won the right to accurate responses by being a thinker in control of his own mind, who mastered all his fears. Thanks to this mastery and control, Hill could demand true and accurate responses from the Devil. In any event, Hill forces the Devil to expose his tricks and wiles—so that we may counter them and avoid the pitfalls in our lives.

Here Begins the *Interview with the Devil*

Q I have uncovered the secret code by which I can pick up your thoughts. I have come to ask you some very plain questions. I demand that you give me direct and truthful answers. Are you ready for the interview, Mr. Devil?

A Yes, I am ready, but you must address me with more respect. During this interview you will address me as "Your Majesty."

Q By what right do you demand such royal respect?

A You should know I control 98 percent of the people of your world. Do you not think that entitles me to rate as royalty?

I had an extremely adverse reaction to hearing the Devil referred to as "Your Majesty" when I first read this interview. Then I realized that Hill probably intended to create just that reaction . . . and I read on. And, of course, the text does not reflect whether Hill might have used an ironic or sarcastic tone when so addressing the Devil.

Q Have you proof of your claim?

A **Yes, plenty of it.**

Q Of what does your proof consist?

A **Of many things. If you want answers, you will address me as "Your Majesty." Some things you will understand; some you will not. In order that you may get my viewpoint, I shall describe myself and correct the false notions people have of me and my place of abode.**

Q That is a fine idea, Your Majesty. Start by telling me where you live. Then describe your physical appearance.

A **My physical appearance? Why, my dear Mr. Earthbound, I have no physical body. I would be handicapped by such an encumbrance as those in which you earthbound creatures live. I consist of negative energy, and I live in the minds of people who fear me. I also occupy one-half of every atom of physical matter and every unit of mental and physical energy. Perhaps you will better understand my nature if I tell you I am the negative portion of the atom.**

Q Oh, I see what you are preparing to claim. You are laying the foundation to say that if it were not for you, there would be no world, no stars, no electrons, no atoms, no human beings, nothing. Is that correct?

A **True! Absolutely true.**

Q Well, if you only occupy one-half of energy and matter, who occupies the other half?

A **The other half is occupied by my opposition.**

Q Opposition? What do you mean?

A **The opposition is what you earthbound call God.**

Q So you have the universe divided up with God. Is that your claim?

A **Not my claim, but the actual fact. Before this interview is finished you will understand why my claim is true. You will also understand why it has to be true, or there could be no world such as yours, no earthbound creatures such as you. I am no beast with a forked tongue and a spiked tail.**

Q But you do control the minds of 98 out of every 100 people. You said so yourself. Who causes all the misery in this 98 percent Devil-controlled world, if you do not?

A **I have not said that I do not cause all the misery of the world. On the other hand, I boast of it. It is my business to represent the negative side of everything, including the thoughts of you earthbound people. How else could I control people? My opposition controls positive thought. I control negative thought.**

Q How do you gain control of the minds of people?

A **Oh, that is easy: I merely move in and occupy the unused space of the human brain. I sow the seeds of negative thought in the minds of people so I can occupy and control the space!**

Q You must have many tricks and devices by which you gain and hold control of the human mind.

A **To be sure, I employ tricks and devices to control human thought. My devices are clever ones too.**

Q Go ahead and describe your clever tricks, Your Majesty.

A One of my cleverest devices for mind control is fear. I plant the seed of fear in the minds of people, and as these seeds germinate and grow, through use, I control the space they occupy. The six most effective fears are the fear of poverty, criticism, ill health, loss of love, old age, and death.

Says the Devil: *"One of my cleverest devices for mind control is fear... the fear of poverty, criticism, ill health, loss of love, old age, and death."*

Q Which of these six fears serves you most often, Your Majesty?

A The first and the last—poverty and death! At one time or another during life I tighten my grip on all people through one or both of these. I plant these fears in the minds of people so deftly that they believe them to be their own creation. I accomplish this end by making people believe I am standing just beyond the entrance gate of the next life, waiting to claim them after death for eternal punishment. Of course I cannot punish anyone, except in that person's own mind, through some form of fear—but fear of the thing which does not exist is just as useful to me as fear of that which does exist. All forms of fear extend the space I occupy in the human mind.

Q Your Majesty, will you explain how you gained this control over human beings?

A The story is too long to be told in a few words. It began over a million years ago, when the first man began to think. Up to that time I had control over all mankind, but enemies of mine discovered the power of positive thought, placed it in the minds of men, and then began a battle on my part to remain in control. So far, I have done quite well by myself, having lost only 2 percent of the people to the opposition.

Q I take it from your answer that men who *think* are your enemies. Is that right?

A It is not *right*, but it is correct.

Q Tell me something more about the world in which you live.

A I live wherever I choose. Time and space do not exist for me. I am a force best described to you as energy. My favorite physical dwelling place, as I have told you, is the minds of the earthbound. I control a part of the brain space of every human being. The amount of space I occupy in each individual's mind depends upon how little and what sort of thinking that person does. As I have told you, I cannot entirely control any person who thinks.

Q You speak of your opposition. What do you mean by that?

A My opponent controls all the positive forces of the world, such as love, faith, hope, and optimism. My opponent also controls the positive factors of all natural law throughout the universe, the forces which keep the earth and the planets and all the stars balanced in their courses, but these forces are meek in comparison with those which operate in the human mind under my control. You see, I do not seek to control stars and planets. I prefer the control of human minds.

Q Where did you acquire your power, and by what means do you add to it?

A **I add to my power by appropriating the mind-power of the earthbound, as they come through the gate at the time of death. Ninety-eight out of every 100 who come back to my plane from the earth plane are taken over by me and their mind-power is added to my being. I get all who come over with any form of fear. You see I am constantly at work, preparing the minds of people before death, so I can appropriate them when they come back to my plane.**

Q Will you tell me how you go about your job of preparing human minds so you can control them?

A **I have countless ways of gaining control of human minds while they are still on the earth plane. My greatest weapon is poverty. I deliberately discourage people from accumulating material wealth because poverty discourages men from thinking and makes them easy prey for me. My next best friend is ill health. An unhealthy body discourages thinking. Then I have countless thousands of workers on earth who aid me in gaining control of human minds. I have these agents placed in every calling. They represent every race and creed, every religion.**

Q Who are your greatest enemies on earth, Your Majesty?

A **All who inspire people to think and act on their own initiative are my enemies. Such men as Socrates, Confucius, Voltaire, Emerson, Thomas Paine, and Abraham Lincoln. And you are not doing me any good either.**

Q Is it true that you use men who have great wealth?

A As I have already told you, poverty is always my friend because it discourages independence of thought and encourages fear in the minds of men. Some wealthy men serve my cause while others do me great damage, depending upon how the wealth is used. The great Rockefeller fortune, for example, is one of my worst enemies.

Q That is interesting, Your Majesty; will you tell me why you fear the Rockefeller fortune more than others?

A The Rockefeller money is being used to isolate and conquer diseases of the physical body, in all parts of the world. Disease has always been one of my most effective weapons. The fear of ill health is second only to the fear of poverty. The Rockefeller money is uncovering new secrets of nature in a hundred different directions, all of which are designed to help men take and keep possession of their own minds. It is encouraging new and better methods of feeding, clothing, and housing people. It is wiping out the slums in the large cities, the places where my favorite allies are found. It is financing campaigns for better government and helping to wipe out dishonesty in politics. It is helping to set higher standards in business practice and encouraging business men to conduct business by the Golden Rule; and that is not doing my cause any good.

Q What about these boys and girls who are said to be on the road to hell? Are you in control of them?

A Well, I can answer that question only with "yes and no." I have corrupted the minds of the young by teaching them to drink and smoke, but they have me baffled through their tendency to think for themselves.

Hill ranges back and forth across the Devil's field of battle. His earlier point about Rockefeller's philanthropy is followed by an explanation of why young people are "on the road to hell." I believe the author is challenging us to hold several ideas in mind at once as he lets the Devil do his dirty work with the hope of confusing us. Look for other examples throughout the book—you'll find them!

Q You say you have corrupted the minds of the young people with liquor and cigarettes. I can understand how liquor might destroy the power of independent thought but do not see what cigarettes have to do with helping your cause.

A You may not know it, but cigarettes break down the power of persistence; they destroy the power of endurance; they destroy the ability to concentrate; they deaden and undermine the imaginative faculty, and help in other ways to keep people from using their minds most effectively.

Do you know I have millions of people, young and old, of both sexes, who smoke two packages of cigarettes a day? That means I have millions of people who are gradually destroying their power of resistance.

One day I shall add to their habit of cigarette smoking other thought-destroying habits, until I shall have gained control of their minds.

Habits come in pairs, triplets, and quadruplets. Any habit which weakens one's will power invites a flock of its relatives to move in and take possession of the mind. The cigarette habit not only lowers the power of resistance and discourages persistence, but it invites looseness in other human relationships.

Q I never thought that cigarettes were a tool of destruction, Your Majesty, but your explanation throws a different light on the subject. How many converts to the habit do you now claim?

A I am proud of my record. Millions are now victims, and the number is increasing daily. Soon I shall have most of the world indulging in the habit. In thousands of families I now have followers of the habit, including every member of the family. Very young boys and girls are beginning to take up the habit. They are learning how to smoke by observing their parents and older brothers and sisters.

Q Which do you consider to be your greater tool for gaining control of human minds—cigarettes or liquor?

A Without hesitation I would say cigarettes. Once I get a young person to join my two-package-a-day club, I have no trouble in inducing that person to take on the habit of liquor, over-indulgence of sex, and all other related habits which destroy independence of thought and action.

Remember, this was written in 1938—long before the addictive nature of tobacco was discovered. Here, as elsewhere, Napoleon Hill is far ahead of his time in some of his medical and sociological opinions.

Q Your Majesty, when I began this interview I had you all wrong. I thought you were a fraud and a fake, but I see now that you are quite real and very powerful.

A **Your apology is accepted, but you need not have bothered. Millions of people have questioned my power, and I got most of them at the gate as they came over.**

I ask no person to believe in me. I prefer that people fear me. I am no beggar! I take what I want by cleverness and force. Begging people to believe is the business of my opposition—not mine.

Q Your Majesty will please pardon my rudeness, but I would not be able to look myself in the face again if I did not tell you, here and now, that you are the damnedest fiend ever to be turned loose on innocent people.

I always had the wrong conception of you. I thought you were kind enough to let people alone while they were living, that you merely tortured their souls after death. Now I learn, from your own brazen confession, that you destroy their right to freedom of thought and cause them to go through a living hell on earth. What do you have to say to that?

A **I get what I want by exercising self-control. It is not so good for my own business, but I suggest you emulate me instead of criticizing me. You call yourself a thinker, and you are. Otherwise you would never have forced this interview on me. But you will never be the sort of thinker that frightens me unless you gain and exercise greater control over your own emotions.**

Q Let us get away from personalities. I came here to learn more about you, not to discuss myself. Please go ahead and tell me of the many tricks you have devised for gaining control of the human mind. What is your most powerful weapon just now?

A That is a difficult question to answer. I have so many devices for entering human minds and controlling them that it is difficult to say which are the most powerful. Right at the moment I am trying to bring about another world war. My friends here in Washington are helping me to involve America in the war. If I can start the world to killing on a wholesale basis, I shall be able to put into operation my favorite device for mind control. It is what you may call mass fear. I used this device to bring about the other World War in 1914. I used it to bring about the economic depression in 1929, and if my opposition had not double-crossed me I would now be in possession of every man, woman, and child in the world. You can see for yourself how near I came to world domination—the thing I have been struggling to attain for thousands of years.

Here the Devil claims to be working with both sides to instigate war, based on his sowing the seeds of fear throughout the world. This is the essence of what has come to be known in our time as terrorism—and the response to it. Through Hill's work the Devil takes credit for not only both World Wars but also the Great Depression . . . it is easy to add the current economic collapse to his list of credits. Both war and economic collapse breed fear in people's minds and are certainly the work of the Devil.

Q Yes, I see your point. Who wouldn't? You are a very ingenious manipulator of the minds of people. Is your devilish business carried on only through people of high position and great influence?

A Oh, no! I use the minds of people in all walks of life. As a matter of fact, I prefer the type of person who makes no pretense of thinking; I can manipulate that sort of person without difficulty. I could not control 98 percent of the people of the world if all people were skilled in thinking for themselves.

Q I am interested in the welfare of those people whom you claim to control. Therefore, I wish you to tell me all of the tricks by which you enter and control their minds. I want a complete confession from you, so begin with your cleverest trick.

A This is suicide you are forcing on me, but I am helpless! So settle down and I will place in your hands the weapon by which millions of your fellow-earthbound will defend themselves against me.

✦ *Chapter Four* ✦

DRIFTING WITH THE DEVIL

Q Tell me first about your most clever trick—the one you use to ensnare the greatest number of people.

A **If you force me to give away this secret, it will mean my loss of millions of people now living and still greater numbers of millions as yet unborn. I beg of you, permit me to pass this one question unanswered.**

Q So His Majesty the Devil fears a mere humble earthbound creature! Is that right?

A **It is not right, but it is true. You have no right to rob me of my most necessary tool of trade. For millions of years I have dominated earthbound creatures through fear and ignorance. Now you come along and would destroy my use of these weapons by forcing me to tell how I use them. Do you not realize that you will break my grip on every person who heeds this confession you are forcing from me? Have you no mercy? Have you no sense of humor? Have you no sportsmanship?**

Q Stop stalling, and start confessing. Who are you to ask mercy of one whom you would destroy if you could? Who are you to talk of sportsmanship and a sense of humor? You, who by your own confession have set up a living hell on earth, where you punish innocent people through their fears and ignorance. As for minding my own business, that is just what I am doing when I force you to tell how you control people through their own minds. My business, if it can be called a business, is helping to unlock the doors of the self-made prisons in which men and women are confined because of the fears you have planted in their minds.

Mr. Earthbound has the power to force the Devil to answer his questions. His own knowledge of independent thought and lack of fear are his weapons to force this confession.

A My greatest weapon over human beings consists of two secret principles by which I gain control of their minds. I will speak first of the principle of habit, through which I silently enter the minds of people. By operating through this principle, I establish (I wish I could avoid using this word) the habit of drifting. When a person begins to drift on any subject, he is headed straight toward the gates of what you earthbound call hell.

Q Describe all the ways in which you induce people to drift. Define the word and tell us exactly what you mean by it.

A I can best define the word "drift" by saying that people who think for themselves never drift, while those who do little or no thinking for themselves are drifters. A drifter is one who permits himself to be influenced and controlled by circumstances outside of his own mind. He would rather let me occupy his mind and do his thinking than go to the trouble of thinking for himself. A drifter is one who accepts whatever life throws in his way without making a protest or putting up a fight. He doesn't know what he wants from life and spends all of his time getting just that. A drifter has lots of opinions, but they are not his own. Most of them are supplied by me.

A drifter is one who is too lazy mentally to use his own brain. That is the reason I can take control of people's thinking and plant my own ideas in their minds.

"Those who do little or no thinking for themselves are drifters. A drifter is one who permits himself to be influenced and controlled by circumstances outside of his own mind."

Q I think I understand what a drifter is. Tell me the exact habits of people by which you induce them to drift through life. Start by telling me when and how you first gain control of a person's mind.

A My control over the mind of a human being is obtained while the person is young. Sometimes I lay the foundation for my control of a mind before the owner of it is born, by manipulating the minds of that person's parents. Sometimes I go further back than this and prepare people for my control through what you earthbound call "physical heredity." You see, therefore, I have two approaches to the mind of a person.

Q Yes. Go on and describe these two doors by which you enter and control the minds of human beings.

A As I have stated, I help to bring people into your world with weak brains by giving to them, before birth, as many as possible of the weaknesses of their ancestors. You call this principle "physical heredity." After people are born I make use of what you earthbound call "environment" as a means of controlling them. This is where the principle of habit enters. The mind is nothing more than the sum total of one's habits! One by one I enter the mind and establish habits, which lead finally to my absolute domination of the mind.

Q Tell me of the most common habits by which you control the minds of people.

A **That is one of my cleverest tricks: I enter the minds of people through thoughts which they believe to be their own. Those most useful to me are fear, superstition, avarice, greed, lust, revenge, anger, vanity, and plain laziness. Through one or more of these I can enter any mind, at any age, but I get my best results when I take charge of a mind while it is young, before its owner has learned how to close any of these nine doors. Then I can set up habits which keep the doors ajar forever.**

Q I am catching on to your methods. Now let us go back to the habit of drifting. Tell us all about that habit since you say it is your cleverest trick in controlling the minds of people.

A **As I said before, I start people drifting during their youth. I induce them to drift through school without knowing what occupation they wish to follow in life. Here I catch the majority of people. Habits are related. Drift in one direction and soon you will be drifting in all directions. I also use environmental habits to give me a definite grip on my victims.**

Q I see. You make it your business to train children in the habit of drifting by inducing them to go through school without aim or purpose. Now tell me of some of your other tricks with which you cause people to become drifters.

A **Well, my second best trick in developing the habit of drifting is one that I put into operation with the aid of parents and public schoolteachers and religious instructors.**

I warn you not to force me to mention this trick. Do not disclose this trick. If you do so, you will be hated by my

co-workers who help me use this trick. If you publish this confession in book form, your book will be barred from the public schools. It will be blacklisted by most of the religious leaders. It will be hidden from children by many parents. The newspapers will not dare to give reviews of your book. Millions of people will hate you for writing the book.

In fact, no one will like you or your book except those who think, and you know how very few there are of this sort! My advice to you is to let me skip the description of my second best trick.

The author knew this opinion would be one of the most controversial aspects of his book. In fact, his wife was so concerned about how it would be received that she made him promise that he would not publish it. In fact, it is only now, well after her death, that the family has agreed to share it with the world. I would encourage you to follow Hill's argument about the public education system and religious teachers and then decide for yourself.

Q So for my own good you wish to withhold the description of your second best trick. No one will like my book except those who think, eh? Very well, go ahead and answer.

A You'll regret this, Mr. Earthbound, but the joke is on you. By this mistake of yours you will divert attention from me to yourself. My co-workers, of whom there are millions, will forget about me and hate you for uncovering my methods.

Q Never mind about me. Tell me all about this second best trick of yours with which you induce people to drift with you to hell.

A My second best trick is not second at all. It is first! It is first because without it I never could gain control of the minds of the youths. Parents, schoolteachers, religious instructors, and many other adults unknowingly serve my purpose by helping me to destroy in children the habit of thinking for themselves. They go about their work in various ways, never suspecting what they are doing to the minds of children or the real cause of the children's mistakes.

Have you ever heard a parent finish a child's sentence? Or seen a parent complete a child's homework? Remember those science fairs at school where it was obvious the kids had a lot of outside "help" with their science projects? Mom and Dad may have "helped" a little too much, but deep down they know that their child appreciates the help and recognizes what great parents they are. Right? Actually, the child may be thinking, "Mom and Dad don't think I can do it on my own . . . so why bother!" Eventually this parental "help" will destroy the child's self-confidence. By allowing children to be truly in charge, parents will help their kids develop the habit of thinking for themselves!

Q I can hardly believe you, Your Majesty. I have always believed that children's best friends were those closest to them, their parents, their school teachers, and their religious instructors. Where would children go for dependable guidance if not to those who have charge of them?

A **That is where my cleverness comes in. There is the exact explanation of how I control 98 percent of the people of the world. I take possession of people during their youth, before they come into possession of their own minds, by using those who are in charge of them. I especially need the help of those who give children their religious instruction, because it is here that I break down independent thought and start people on the habit of drifting, by confusing their minds with unprovable ideas concerning a world of which they know nothing. It is here also that I plant in the minds of children the greatest of all fears—the fear of hell!**

Q I understand that it is easy for you to frighten children with threats of hell, but how do you continue to make them fear you and your hell after they grow up and learn to think for themselves?

A **Children grow up, but they do not always learn to think for themselves! Once I capture the mind of a child, through fear, I weaken that child's ability to reason and to think for himself, and that weakness goes with the child all through life.**

Q Is that not taking unfair advantage of a human being by contaminating his mind before he comes into full possession of it?

A **Everything is fair that I can use to further my ends. I have no foolish limitations of right and wrong. Might is right with me. I use every known human weakness to gain and keep control of the human mind.**

Q I understand your devilish nature! Now let us get back to further discussion of your methods of inducing people to drift to hell here on earth. From your confession I see that you take charge of children while their minds are young and pliable. Tell me more of how you use parents, teachers, and religious leaders to ensnare people into drifting.

A One of my favorite tricks is to coordinate the efforts of parents and religious instructors so they work together in helping me to destroy the children's power to think for themselves. I use many religious instructors to undermine the courage and power of independent thought of children, by teaching them to fear me; but I use parents to aid the religious leaders in this great work of mine.

Q How do parents help religious leaders destroy their children's power to think for themselves? I never heard of such a monstrosity!

A I accomplish this through a very clever trick. I cause the parents to teach their children to believe as the parents do in connection with religion, politics, marriage, and other important subjects. In this way, as you can see, when I gain control of the mind of a person I can easily perpetuate the control by causing that person to help me fasten it upon the minds of his offspring.

Q In what other ways do you use parents to convert children into drifters?

A I cause children to become drifters by following the example of their parents, most of whom I have already taken over and bound eternally to my cause. In some parts of the

world I gain mastery over children's minds and subdue their will power in exactly the same way that men break and subdue animals of lower intelligence. It makes no difference to me how a child's will is subdued, as long as it fears something. I will enter its mind through that fear and limit the child's power to think independently.

The Devil will enter a child's mind through fear and then limit the child's power to think independently. I can remember the many religious leaders I have known in the past and instantly divide them between fear-based instructors and faith-based instructors. In fact, I still get a chill from reliving the "fire and brimstone" of some of the fear-based sermons I heard as a child. In contrast, I remember the uplifted feeling of hope and courage from the faith-based sermons. Hill's words of wisdom certainly ring true for me. Does fear then paralyze independent thought?

Q It seems that you go out of your way to keep people from thinking?

A Yes. Accurate thought is death to me. I cannot exist in the minds of those who think accurately. I do not mind people thinking as long as they think in terms of fear, discouragement, hopelessness, and destructiveness. When they begin to think in constructive terms of faith, courage, hope, and definiteness of purpose, they immediately become allies of my opposition and are therefore lost to me.

Q I am beginning to understand how you gain control of the minds of children through the help of their parents and religious instructors, but I do not see how the schoolteachers help you in this damnable work.

A Schoolteachers help me gain control of the minds of children not so much by what they teach the children as because of what they do not teach them. The entire public school system is so administered that it helps my cause by teaching children almost everything except how to use their own minds and think independently. I live in fear that someday some courageous person will reverse the present system of school teaching and deal my cause a death blow by allowing the students to become the instructors, using those who now serve as teachers only as guides to help the children establish ways and means of developing their own minds from within. When that time comes, the schoolteachers will no longer belong to my staff.

Here is the essence of Hill's critique of public education, written in 1938. Do you agree with him? Think of young children during kindergarten and first grade. They are enthusiastic and volunteer for everything, raising their hands and excited to learn. Now fast-forward ten years, and think about those same children as high school students—the ones sitting in the back of the class, never making eye contact with adults, and absolutely never volunteering or asking a question. They have disengaged from the learning process. What happened to these children? Ten years of schooling. They perceive that to make an error will subject them to ridicule and scorn. So they cease to participate in order to protect themselves. They are taught that the solutions to all

problems and conflicts lie not in their own hands and minds, but in the hands and mind of the teacher—the representative of the authorities. To act independently in the face of conflict brings swift rebuke and reprisal from the teacher. The children are thus discouraged from independent thought and indoctrinated with the concept that they are incapable of resolving their own problems. While there are many excellent teachers, Hill's critique seems validated by the state of education today. If you agree with Hill, what do you think we can do about it? One thing we should do is to seek out those teachers and schools who encourage independent thought in their students and applaud them for their courage!

Q I was under the impression that the purpose of all schooling was to help children to think.

A That may be the purpose of schooling, but the system in most of the schools of the world does not carry out the purpose. School children are taught not to develop and use their own minds, but to adopt and use the thoughts of others. This sort of schooling destroys the capacity for independent thought, except in a few rare cases where children rely so definitely upon their own will power that they refuse to allow others to do their thinking. Accurate thought is the business of my opposition, not mine!

Q What relationship, if any, has your opposition with the homes, the churches, and the schools? Your reply to this question should be interesting.

A Here is where I make use of some more of my clever tricks.

I cause it to appear that everything done by the parents, the schoolteachers, and the religious instructors is being done by my opposition.

This diverts attention from me while I manipulate the minds of the young. When religious instructors try to teach children the virtues of my opposition, they generally do so by frightening them with my name. That is all I ask of them. I kindle the flame of fear into proportions which destroy the child's power to think accurately. In the public schools the teachers further my cause by keeping the children so busy cramming non-essential information into their minds they have no opportunity to think accurately or to analyze correctly the things their instructors teach them.

Q Do you claim, for your cause, all those who are bound by the habit of drifting?

A **No. Drifting is only one of my tricks through which I take over the power of independent thought. Before a drifter becomes my permanent property, I must lead him on and ensnare him with another trick. I will tell you about this other trick after I finish describing my methods of converting people into drifters.**

Q Do you mean you have a method by which you can cause people to drift so far away from self-determination that they can never save themselves?

A **Yes, a definite method: And it is so effective it never fails.**

Q Do I understand you to claim your method is so powerful your opposition cannot reclaim those whom you have permanently ensnared through drifting?

A I claim just that! Do you think I would control so many people if my opposition could prevent me? Nothing can stop me from controlling people except people themselves.

Nothing can stop me except the power of accurate thought. People who think accurately do not drift on any subject. They recognize the power of their own minds. Moreover, they take over that power and yield it to no person or influence.

Q Go ahead and tell me more of the methods by which you cause people to drift to hell with you!

A I cause people to drift on every subject through which I can control independent thought and action. Take the subject of health, for example. I cause most people to eat too much food and the wrong sort of food. This leads to indigestion and destroys the power of accurate thought. If the public schools and the churches taught children more about proper eating, they would do my cause irreparable damage.

Marriage: I cause men and women to drift into marriage without plan or purpose designed to convert the relationship into harmony. Here is one of my most effective methods of converting people into the habit of drifting. I cause married people to bicker and nag one another over money matters. I cause them to quarrel over the bringing up of their children. I engage them in unpleasant controversies over their intimate relationships and in disagreements over friends and social activities. I keep them so busy finding fault with one another that they never have time to do anything else long enough to break the habit of drifting.

Occupation: I teach people to become drifters by causing them to drift out of school into the first job they can find, with no definite aim or purpose except to make a living. Through this trick I keep millions of people in fear of poverty all their lives. Through this fear I lead them slowly but surely onward until they reach the point beyond which no individual ever has broken the drifting habit.

Savings: I cause people to spend freely and to save sparingly or not at all, until I take complete control of them through their fear of poverty.

Environment: I cause people to drift into inharmonious and unpleasant environments in the home, in their places of occupation, in their relationship with relatives and acquaintances, and to remain there until I claim them through the habit of drifting.

Dominating Thoughts: I cause people to drift into the habit of thinking negative thoughts. This leads to negative acts and involves people in controversies and fills their minds with fears, thus paving the way for me to enter and control their minds. When I move in, I do so by appealing to people through negative thoughts which they believe to be their own. I plant the seeds of negative thought in the minds of people through the pulpit, the newspapers, the moving pictures, the radio, and all other popular methods of appeal to the mind. I cause people to allow me to do their thinking for them because they are too lazy and too indifferent to think for themselves.

Q I conclude from what you say that drifting and procrastination are the same. Is that true?

A Yes, that is correct. Any habit which causes one to procrastinate—to put off reaching a definite decision—leads to the habit of drifting.

Says the Devil: *"I cause people to allow me to do their thinking for them because they are too lazy and too indifferent to think for themselves."*

✦ ✦ ✦ ✦ ✦ ✦ ✦ ✦ ✦ ✦

Laziness + Indifference = Procrastination = Drifting.

This describes a true drifter as defined by Hill. Since I have been a true procrastinator for most of my life, this hits a little too close to home for me. I like to use the excuse that I work best under pressure—but that is all it is: an excuse for why I procrastinate. Can you think of examples in your own life when laziness and indifference led you off your path to success? When an opportunity slipped through your fingers because you were too slow to seize it in time?

Q Is man the only creature who drifts?

A Yes. All other creatures move in response to definite laws of nature. Man alone defies nature's laws and drifts when he wills.

Everything outside the minds of men is controlled by my opposition, by laws so definite that drifting is impossible. I control the minds of men solely because of their habit of drifting, which is only another way of saying that I control the minds of men only because they neglect or refuse to control and use their own minds.

Q This is getting to be pretty deep stuff for a mere human being. Let us get back to the discussion of something less abstract. Please tell me how this drifting habit affects people in the everyday walks of life and tell me in terms the average person can understand.

A **I would prefer to keep this interview up among the stars!**

Q No doubt you would. That would save you from being exposed. But let us come back to earth. Tell me now what drifting is doing to us as a nation here in the United States.

A **Frankly, I may as well tell you that I hate the United States as only the Devil can hate.**

Q That is interesting. What is the cause of this hatred?

A **The cause was born on July 4, 1776, when fifty-six men signed a document which destroyed my chances of controlling the nation. You know that document as the Declaration of Independence. Had it not been for the influence of that damnable document, I would now have a dictator running the country and I would stop this right to free speech and independent thought that is threatening my rule on earth.**

Q Am I to understand from what you say that nations controlled by self-appointed dictators belong in your camp?

A **There are no self-appointed dictators. I appoint them all. Moreover, I manipulate them and direct them in their work. Nations run by my dictators know what they want and take it by force. Look what I have done through Mussolini in Italy! Look what I am doing through Hitler in Germany. Look what I am doing through Stalin in Russia. My dictators run those nations for me because the people have been subdued through the habit of drifting. My dictators do no drifting. That is why they rule for me the millions of people under their control.**

Q What would happen if Mussolini, Stalin, and Hitler turned traitors and disavowed you and your rule?

A **That will not happen because I have them too well bribed. I am paying each of them with the sop of his own vanity, by making him believe he is acting on his own account. That is another trick of mine.**

Q Let us come back to the United States and learn something of what you are doing to convert people into the habit of drifting.

A **Right now I am paving the way for a dictatorship by sowing the seeds of fear and uncertainty in the minds of the people.**

Q Through whom are you carrying on your work?

A **Mainly through the President. I am destroying his influence with the people by causing him to drift on the question of a working agreement between employers and their employees. If I can induce him to drift for another year, he will be so thoroughly discredited I can hand over the country to a dictator. If the President continues to drift, I will paralyze personal freedom in the United States just as I destroyed it in Spain, Italy, Germany, and England.**

In 1938 when Hill was writing this manuscript, the president was Franklin D. Roosevelt. Are the Devil's comments applicable today? Do you think Hill might write the same words today as he wrote seventy years ago?

Q What you say leads me to the conclusion that drifting is a weakness which inevitably ends in failure, whether among individuals or nations. Is that your claim?

A Drifting is the most common cause of failure in every walk of life. I can control anyone whom I can induce to form the habit of drifting on any subject. The reason for this is two-fold. First, the drifter is just so much putty in my hands, to be molded into whatever pattern I choose, because drifting destroys the power of individual initiative. Second, the drifter cannot get help from my opposition, because the opposition is not attracted to anything so soft and useless.

Q Is that why a few people are wealthy while the majority of people are poor?

A That is exactly the reason. Poverty, like physical illness, is a contagious disease. You find it always among the drifters, never among those who know what they want and are determined to get just that! It may mean something to you when I call your attention to the fact that the non-drifters, whom I do not control, and those who possess most of the wealth of the world, happen to be the same people.

Q I have always understood that money was the root of all evil, that the poor and the meek would inherit heaven, while the wealthy would pass into your hands. What have you to say of that claim?

A Men who know how to get the material things of life generally know how to keep out of the hands of the Devil as well. The ability to acquire things is contagious. Drifters acquire nothing except that which no one else wants. If more people had definite aims and stronger desires for material and spiritual riches, I would have fewer victims.

The actual verse of the Bible talks about the "love of money," not money itself:
"For the love of money is the root of all kinds of evil."
1 Timothy 6:10

Q I assume, from what you say, that you do not claim fellowship with the industrial leaders. Evidently they are not friends of yours.

A Friends of mine? I'll tell you what sort of friends of mine they are. They have belted the entire country with good roads, thus bringing into close communion the people of both city and country. They have converted ores into steel, with which they have built the skeletons of great skyscrapers. They have harnessed electrical power and converted it into a thousand uses, all designed to give man time to think. They have provided through the automobile personal transportation to the humblest citizen, thus giving to everyone the freedom of travel. They have provided every home with instantaneous news of what is happening in all parts of the world through the aid of the radio.

...and now television, smart phone, satellite, and Internet!

They have reared libraries in every city, town, and hamlet and have filled them with books giving to all who read a complete outline of the most useful knowledge mankind has gathered from his experiences. They have given the humblest citizen the right to express his own opinion on any subject, anytime, anywhere, without fear of molestation, and they have seen to it that every citizen may help make his own laws, levy his own taxes, and manage his own country through the ballot. These are but some of the things the industrial leaders have done to give every citizen the privilege of becoming a non-drifter. Do you think these men have helped my cause?

Q Who are some of the present-day non-drifters over whom you have no control?

A I have control over no non-drifter, present or past. I control the weak, not those who think for themselves.

Q Go ahead and describe a typical drifter. Give your description point by point so I can recognize a drifter when I see him.

A The first thing you will notice about a drifter is his total lack of a major purpose in life.

He will be conspicuous by his lack of self-confidence.

He will never accomplish anything requiring thought and effort.

He spends all he earns and more too, if he can get credit.

He will be sick or ailing from some real or imaginary cause, and calling to high heaven if he suffers the least physical pain.

He will have little or no imagination.

He will lack enthusiasm and initiative to begin anything he is not forced to undertake, and he will plainly express his weakness by taking the line of least resistance whenever he can do so.

He will be ill-tempered and lacking in control over his emotions.

His personality will be without magnetism and it will not attract other people.

He will have opinions on everything but accurate knowledge of nothing.

He may be jack of all trades but good at none.

He will neglect to cooperate with those around him, even those on whom he must depend for food and shelter.

He will make the same mistake over and over again, never profiting by failure.

He will be narrow-minded and intolerant on all subjects, ready to crucify those who may disagree with him.

He will expect everything of others but be willing to give little or nothing in return.

He may begin many things but he will complete nothing.

He will be loud in his condemnation of his government, but he will never tell you definitely how it can be improved.

He will never reach decisions on anything if he can avoid it, and if he is forced to decide he will reverse himself at the first opportunity.

He will eat too much and exercise too little.

He will take a drink of liquor if someone else will pay for it.

He will gamble if he can do it "on the cuff."

He will criticize others who are succeeding in their chosen calling.

In brief, the drifter will work harder to get out of thinking than most others work in earning a good living.

He will tell a lie rather than admit his ignorance on any subject.

If he works for others, he will criticize them to their backs and flatter them to their faces.

Q You have given me a graphic description of the drifter. Please now describe the non-drifter so that I may recognize him on sight.

A The first sign of a non-drifter is this: He is always engaged in doing something definite, through some well-organized plan which is definite. He has a major goal in life toward which he is always working, and many minor goals, all of which lead toward his central scheme.

The tone of his voice, the quickness of his step, the sparkle in his eyes, the quickness of his decisions clearly mark him as a person who knows exactly what he wants and is determined to get it, no matter how long it may take or what price he must pay.

If you ask him questions, he gives you direct answers and never falls back on evasions or resorts to subterfuge.

He extends many favors to others, but accepts favors sparingly or not at all.

He will be found up front whether he is playing a game or fighting a war.

If he does not know the answers he will say so frankly.

He has a good memory; never offers an alibi for his shortcomings.

He never blames others for his mistakes no matter if they deserve the blame.

He used to be known as a go-getter, but in modern times he is called a go-giver. You will find him running the biggest business in town, living on the best street, driving the best automobile, and making his presence felt wherever he happens to be.

He is an inspiration to all who come into contact with his mind.

The major distinguishing feature of the non-drifter is this: He has a mind of his own and uses it for all purposes.

The non-drifter
"has a mind of his own and uses it for all purposes."

+ + + + + + + + + + +

Can you think of someone you know who fits this description? Is that person a non-drifter?

Q Is the non-drifter born with some mental, physical, or spiritual advantage not available to the drifter?

A **No. The major difference between the drifter and the non-drifter is something equally available to both. It is simply the prerogative right of each to use his own mind and think for himself.**

Q What brief message would you send to the typical drifter if you wished to cure him of this evil habit?

A **I would admonish him to wake up and give!**

Q Give what?

A **Some form of service useful to as many people as possible.**

Q So the non-drifter is supposed to give, is he?

A **Yes, if he expects to get! And he must give before he gets!**

Q Some people doubt that you exist.

A **I wouldn't worry about that if I were you. Those who are ready to be converted from the habit of drifting will recognize the authenticity of this interview by its soundness of counsel. The others are not worth the trouble it would take to convert them.**

Q Why do you not try to stop me from publishing this confession I am wringing from you?

A **Because that would be the surest of all ways to guarantee you will publish it. I have a better plan than trying to suppress publication of my confession. I will urge you to go ahead** with the publication, then sit back and watch you suffer when some of my faithful drifters begin to make things hot for you. I will not need to deny your story. My followers will do that for me—see if they don't.

Knowing that indeed this book was not published for more than seventy years after Hill wrote these words, I am intrigued and anxious to learn what else he will reveal! There are plenty of fireworks still ahead...

✦ *Chapter Five* ✦

THE CONFESSION CONTINUES

Q IF THIS CONFESSION OF YOURS STOPPED right here your statement would be sound, but fortunately for millions of your victims who will gain their release because of your confession, this interview will continue until you have supplied me with the weapon by which you will eventually be restrained from domination of people through their fears and superstitions. Remember, Your Majesty, your confession has just begun. After I wring from you a description of the methods by which you control people, I will force you also to give the formula by which your control can be broken at will.

It is true I shall not remain here long enough to defeat you, but the published word I leave behind me will be deathless because it will consist of truth! You fear the opposition of no individual because you know it will be short, but you do fear truth. You fear truth and nothing else, for the reason it is slowly but definitely giving human beings freedom from all manner of fear. Without the weapon of fear you would be helpless and entirely unable to control any human being! Is that true or false?

"It is true I shall not remain here long enough to defeat you, but the published word I leave behind me will be deathless because it will consist of truth!"

Indeed, Napoleon Hill passed away in 1970, and this work being published in 2011 becomes deathless.

A I have no alternative but to admit that what you say is true.

Q Now that we understand each other, let us go ahead with your confession. But before we continue, I may as well take time out to do a little boasting on my own account, now that you have had your fling at it. I will confine myself to one question, the answer to which will give me all the satisfaction I want. Is it not true that you control only the minds of those who have allowed the drifting habit to be fixed upon them?

A **Yes, that is true. I have already admitted this truth in a dozen or more different ways. Why do you tantalize me by repeating the question?**

Q There is power in repetition. I am forcing you to repeat the highlights of your confession in as many different ways as possible so your victims may check this interview and determine its soundness by their own experiences with you. That is one of my little tricks. Do you approve of my method?

A **You couldn't be setting a trap for me for the purpose of doing some more boasting, could you?**

Q I am asking the questions and you are doing the answering! Go ahead now and confess why you are powerless to stop me from forcing this confession from you. I want your confession for aid and comfort to victims of yours whom I intend to release from your control the moment they read your confession.

A **I am powerless to influence or control you because you have found the secret approach to my kingdom. You know that I exist only in the minds of people who have fears. You know that I control only the drifters who neglect to use their own minds. You know that my hell is here on earth and not in the** world that comes after death. And you know also that drifters supply all the fire I use in my hell. You know that I am a principle or form of energy which expresses the negative side of matter and energy, and that I am not a person with a forked tongue and a spiked tail. You have become my master because you have mastered all your fears. Lastly, you know that you can release all of my earthbound victims whom you contact, and this definite knowledge is the blow with which you will deal me the greatest damage.

I cannot control you because you have discovered your own mind and you have taken charge of it. There now, Mr. Earthbound, that confession should feed your vanity to the bursting point.

Says the Devil: ***"I cannot control you because you have discovered your own mind and you have taken charge of it. This definite knowledge is the blow with which you will deal me the greatest damage."***

Q That last dart was unnecessary. Knowledge of the sort I have used to master you does not contaminate itself with vulgar indulgence in vanity. Truth is the one, and only, thing in the world that can stand ridicule. Now let us continue with your confession. What is wrong with the principle of flattery? You use it, do you not?

A Do I use it? Man alive! Flattery is one of my most useful weapons. With this deadly instrument I slay the big ones and the little ones.

Q Your admission interests me. Go ahead now and tell me how you make use of flattery.

A **I make use of it in so many ways it is difficult to know where to begin. I warn you, before I answer in detail, that publishing my answers will bring down an avalanche of ridicule on your head for bringing up the question.**

Q I'll take the responsibility. Proceed.

A **Well, I may as well here admit that you have stumbled onto the major secret of how I convert people to the habit of drifting!**

Q That is a startling admission. Go ahead with your confession, and stick strictly to this subject of flattery. No more side remarks and no more facetiousness for the present. Tell me all about your use of flattery in gaining control over people.

A **Flattery is a bait of incomparable value to all who wish to gain control over others. It has powerful pulling qualities because it operates through two of the most common human weaknesses: vanity and egotism. There is a certain amount of vanity and egotism in everyone. In some people these qualities are so pronounced they literally serve as a rope by which one may be bound. The best of all ropes is flattery.**

Flattery is the chief bait through which men seduce women. Sometimes—in fact, frequently—women use the same bait to gain control of men, especially men who cannot be mastered through sex appeal. I teach its use to both men and women. Flattery is the chief bait with which my agents weave their way into the confidence of people from whom they procure information needed to carry on warfare.

Wherever anyone stops to feed his vanity on flattery, I move in and begin to build another drifter. Non-drifters are not easily flattered. I inspire people to use flattery in every human relationship where its use is possible because those who are influenced by it become easy victims of the drifting habit.

Says the Devil: *"Flattery is the chief bait through which men seduce women."*

Q Can you control anyone who is amenable to flattery?

A Very easily. As I have already told you, flattery is of major importance in alluring people into the habit of drifting.

Q At what age are people most susceptible to flattery?

A Age has nothing to do with one's susceptibility to flattery. People respond to it, in one way or another, from the time they become conscious of their own existence until they die.

Q Through what motive can women be most easily flattered?

A Their vanity. Tell a woman she is pretty or that she wears clothes well.

Q What motive is most effective in harpooning men?

A Egotism, with a capital E! Tell a man he has a strong Herculean body or that he is a great business tycoon, and he will purr like a cat and smile like an opossum! After that you know what happens.

Q Are all men like that?

A **Oh, no. Two out of every hundred have their egotism so thoroughly under control that even an expert flatterer couldn't get under their skins with a double-edged butcher knife.**

Q How does a cunning woman apply her art of flattery in attracting men?

A **Great heavens, man, do I have to draw a picture of her method for you? Have you no imagination?**

Q Oh, yes, I have imagination enough, Your Majesty, but I am thinking of the poor dupes of the world who need to understand the exact technique with which they may be flattered into the habit of drifting. Go on and tell us how a woman can harpoon rich and presumably smart men.

A **This is a devilish trick to play on women, but since you demand the information I am helpless to withhold it. Women influence men through a technique consisting, first, of ability to inject soft, cooing baby tones into their voices, and, second, by closing their eyes into a half-closed position which registers hypnotism in connection with the flattery of men.**

I am sure there are a few women agitated by this; in fact, I was at first. Roll your eyes, and keep going... there is truth here!

Q Is that all there is to the business of flattery?

A No, that is only the technique. Then comes the motive a woman uses as a lure. The type of woman you perhaps have in mind never sells a man herself or anything she can give him. Instead she sells him his own egotism!

Q Is that all that women use when they wish to flatter men?

A That is the most effective thing they use. It works when sex appeal fails!

Q So I am to believe that big, strong, smart men can be wound up and manipulated through flattery, just as if they were so much putty? Is that possible?

A Is it possible? It is happening every minute of the day. Moreover, unless they are non-drifters, the bigger they come, the harder they fall when the expert flatterer moves in on them.

Q Tell me of some of your other tricks with which you cause people to drift in life.

A One of my most effective devices is failure! The majority of people begin to drift as soon as they meet with opposition, and not one out of ten thousand will keep on trying after failing two or three times.

Q So it is your business to induce people to fail whenever you can. Is that correct?

A You have it right. Failure breaks down one's morale, destroys self-confidence, subdues enthusiasm, dulls imagination, and drives away definiteness of purpose.

Without these qualities no one can permanently succeed in any undertaking. The world has produced thousands of inventors with ability superior to that of the late Thomas A. Edison. But these men have never been heard of, while the name of Edison will go marching on because Edison converted failure into a stepping stone to achievement while the others used it as an alibi for not producing results.

Q Is the capacity to surmount failure without being discouraged one of Henry Ford's chief assets?

A Yes, and this same quality is the chief asset of every man who attains outstanding success in any calling.

The "capacity to surmount failure without being discouraged" is "the chief asset of every man who attains outstanding success in any calling."

✦ ✦ ✦ ✦ ✦ ✦ ✦ ✦ ✦ ✦

In the book *Three Feet from Gold* my co-author and I interviewed more than thirty-five of today's top leaders, not about their successes but about their toughest moments and how they persevered to achieve great success. For example, Julie Krone, the first woman ever inducted into the Thoroughbred Hall of Fame, with 3,704 victories under her reins, described her struggles at the beginning of her career as a jockey. Many of the horse owners simply would not hire a woman jockey. She said her motto of perseverance was, "Keep showing up!" She said, "I discovered if I showed up every day and did my best, eventually they'd put me on a horse just to get rid of me." The rest is history. Julie was named as one of the toughest athletes of all time by *USA Today*.

Q That statement covers lots of territory, Your Majesty. Do you not wish to modify it or tone it down a bit for the sake of accuracy?

_A_ No modification is necessary because the claim is none too broad. Search accurately into the lives of men and women who achieve enduring success and you will find, without exception, that their success has been in exact proportion to the extent that they surmounted failure.

The life of every successful person loudly acclaims that which every true philosopher knows: "Every failure brings with it the seed of an equivalent success."

But the seed will not germinate and grow under the influence of a drifter. It springs to life only when it is in the hands of one who recognizes that most failures are only temporary defeat, and who never, under any circumstances, accepts defeat as an excuse for drifting.

Q If I understand you correctly, you claim there is virtue in failure. That does not seem reasonable. Why do you try to induce people to fail if there is virtue in failure?

_A_ There is no inconsistency in my claims. The appearance of inconsistency is due to your lack of understanding. Failure is a virtue only when it does not lead one to quit trying and begin drifting. I induce as many people as I can to fail as often as possible for the reason that not one out of ten thousand will keep on trying after failing two or three times. I am not concerned about the few who convert failures into stepping stones because they belong to my opposition anyway. They are the non-drifters and therefore they are beyond my reach.

Q Your explanation clears up the matter. Now go ahead and tell me of some of your other tricks with which you allure people into drifting.

"Edison converted failure into a stepping stone to achievement while the others used it as an alibi for not producing results."

✦ ✦ ✦ ✦ ✦ ✦ ✦ ✦ ✦ ✦

How are you dealing with failure in your life?

A One of my most effective tricks is known to you as propaganda. This is the instrument of greatest value to me in setting people to murdering one another under the guise of war.

The cleverness of this trick consists mainly of the subtlety with which I use it.

I mix propaganda with the news of the world. I have it taught in public and private schools. I see that it finds its way into the pulpit. I color moving pictures with it. I see that it enters every home where there is a radio. I inject it into billboard, newspaper, and radio advertising. I spread it in every place of business where people work. I use it to fill the divorce courts and I make it serve to destroy business and industry.

It is my chief instrument for starting runs on banks. My propagandists cover the world so thoroughly that I can start epidemics of disease, turn loose the dogs of war, or throw business into a panic at will.

Q If you can do all that you claim with propaganda, it is little wonder that we have wars and business depressions. Give me a simple description of what you mean by the term "propaganda." Just what is it and how does it work? I wish to know particularly how you cause people to drift through the use of this devilish device.

A Propaganda is any device, plan, or method by which people can be influenced without knowing that they are being influenced, or the source of the influence.

Propaganda is used in business for the purpose of discouraging competition. Employers use it to gain advantage over their employees. The employees retaliate by using it to gain advantage over their employers. In fact, it is used so universally and through such a smooth and beautiful streamlined technique that it looks harmless even when it is detected.

Q I suppose some of your boys are now engaged in preparing the minds of the American people to drift into some form of dictatorship. Tell me how they work.

A Yes! Millions of my boys are preparing Americans to become Hitlerized. My best boys are working through politics and labor organization. We intend to take over the country with ballots instead of bullets. Americans are so sensitive they would never stand the shock of seeing their form of government changed with the aid of machine guns and tank cars. So our propaganda boys are serving them a diet they will swallow, by stirring up strife between employers and employees and turning the government against business and industry. When propaganda has done its work thoroughly, one of my boys will move in as dictator and the Nine Old Men on your Supreme Court with their silly notions of the Constitution will move out!

Everyone will be given a job or fed from the government treasury. When men's bellies are filled, they drift freely with one who does the filling. Hungry men get out from under control.

In 1938, one of the Devil's tools for "Hitlerizing" America was "turning the government against business and industry" and feeding the populace from the government treasury. Is that still the case today? Is the Devil succeeding? Were Napoleon Hill to interview the Devil today, the Devil might well gloat over the so-called "entitlement" programs now in place or proposed and crow over the government's increasing involvement in independent businesses, such as the automotive and financial industries.

Q I have often wondered who invented the clever trick which you call propaganda. From what you tell me of its source and nature I understand why it is so deadly. Only one as clever as Your Majesty could have invented such a device with which to dull the reason, dethrone the will, and lure men into drifting.

Why do you not use your powerful propaganda to gain control of your victims instead of subduing them through fear and annihilating them through warfare?

A What is fear of the Devil except propaganda? You have not observed my technique very carefully or you would have seen that I am the world's greatest propagandist! I never attain an end by direct, open means which I can achieve through subterfuge and subtlety. What do you suppose I am using, when I plant negative ideas in the minds of men and gain control of them

through what they believe to be their own ideas? What would you call that except the cleverest of all forms of propaganda?

Q Surely you are not going to tell me that you destroy people through their own help without their realizing what you are doing?

A **That is exactly what I wish you to understand. Moreover, I will show you exactly how the trick is performed.**

Q Now we are getting somewhere. Exactly how do you convert human beings into propagandists and lure them into self-imprisonment? Give me the story with all its lurid details. This is the most important part of your confession and I am consumed with eagerness to gain control of your secret. I can hardly blame you for stalling about answering my question because you know so well that your answer will snatch millions of innocent victims from your control. You also know that your answer will protect other countless millions of yet unborn people from being victimized by you. It is little wonder you are hedging about answering.

A **Your deductions are correct. This part of my confession will do me more damage than all the remainder of it.**

Q Stating your headache in a better way, this part of your confession will save more millions of people from your control than all the remainder of it.

A **All I can say is that you have me in a hell of a situation!**

Q Now you shall know how the millions of your victims feel. Let's have it.

A I make my first entry into an individual's mind by bribing him.

Q What do you use as a bribe?

A I use many things, all of them pleasant things the individual covets. I use the same sort of bribes that individuals use when they bribe one another. That is, I use for bribes the things people most want. My best bribes are these:

- Love
- The thirst for sex expression
- Covetousness for money
- The obsessive desire to gain something for nothing—gambling
- Vanity in women, egotism in men

In today's environment, clearly both women and men can fall victim to both vanity and egotism.

- Desire to be the master of others
- Desire for intoxicants and narcotics
- Desire for self-expression through words and deeds
- Desire to imitate others
- Desire for perpetuation of life after death
- Desire to be a hero or heroine
- Desire for physical food

Q That is an imposing list of bribes, Your Majesty. Do you use others?

A **Yes, plenty of them, but these are my favorites. Through some combination of them I can enter the mind of any human being at will at any age from birth until death.**

Q You mean that these bribes are the keys with which you can silently unlock the door to any mind you choose?

A **That is exactly what I mean and I can do it too.**

Q What happens when you enter the mind of a person who is not yet in the habit of drifting, but belongs in the 98 percent class as a potential drifter?

A **I go to work immediately to occupy as much of that person's mind as I can master. If the individual's greatest weakness is the desire for money, I begin to dangle coins before him, figuratively speaking. I intensify his desire and induce him to go after money. Then when he gets near it I snatch it away from him.**

This is an old trick of mine. After the trick has been repeated a few times, the poor fellow gives in and quits. Then I take over a little more space in his mind and fill it with the fear of poverty. That is one of my best mind-fillers.

Q Yes, I admit your method is very clever, but what happens if the victim fools you and gets his hands on a lot of money? You don't fill his mind with fear of poverty then, do you?

A **No, I don't. I take over the space by filling it with something which serves my purpose just as well. If my victim converts his** desire for money into large sums, I start over-feeding him with the things he can buy with it. For example, I cause him to stuff himself with rich foods. This slows down his thinking capacity, endangers his heart, and starts him on the road to drifting.

Then I pester him with intestinal poisoning through the surplus food he eats. That also slows down his thinking and gives him a nasty disposition.

Q What if the victim is not a glutton? What other follies can you induce him to pick up that lead to drifting?

A **If the victim is a male I can usually snare him through his sex appetite. Over-indulgence in sex starts more men to drifting toward failure than all other causes combined.**

Q So food and sex are two of your sure-fire baits! Is that correct?

A **Yes. With these two lures I can take over a majority of my victims, and then there is the desire for money.**

Q I am beginning to think that wealth is more dangerous than poverty, if your story is to be believed.

A **That altogether depends upon who has the wealth and how it was acquired.**

Q What has the manner in which money is acquired to do with its being a blessing or a curse?

A **Everything. If you don't believe me, take a look at those who acquire a large amount of money quickly, without time to get wisdom along with it, and observe how they use it.**

Why, do you suppose, rich men's sons seldom equal the achievements of their fathers? I'll tell you why. It is because they have been deprived of the self-discipline which comes from being forced to work.

Look into the records of moving picture stars or athletes who suddenly find themselves in possession of big money and hero worship and praise from the public. Observe how quickly I move in and take them over in many cases, mainly through sex, gambling, food, and liquor. With these I catch and control the biggest and the best of people as soon as they get their hands on big money.

Think of the countless athletes who have become mega-celebrities only to crash and burn from their fast money and fame . . . and then think of the millions of young people who looked up to them! Think of lottery winners who end up losing all their money within just a few years after they win the lottery . . . could it be from drifting . . . a fall-out from gambling? Could these cycles be orchestrated by the Devil?

Q What about those who acquire money slowly, by rendering some form of useful service? Are they easily snared too?

A Oh, I get them all right, but I generally have to change my bait. Some of them want one thing and others want something else.

Where my purpose is best served I see to it that they get what they want most, but I manage to wrap in the package something they don't want. The thing I give them is the definite thing that makes them drifters. Do you see how I work?

Q And very clever work it is. You lure people on through their natural desires, but you slip your deadly poison into the object of those desires wherever you can.

A **Now you are catching on. You see, I play both ends against the middle, so to speak.**

Q From all you say I infer that you cannot induce a non-drifter to help you gain control of his mind by baiting him with your bribes. Is that correct?

A **That is exactly correct. I can—and I do—interest non-drifters in my bribes, because I use for the purpose of bribery the things all people naturally desire, but the non-drifter resembles a fish that steals the bait from your hook but refuses to take the hook.**

The non-drifter takes from life whatever he wants, but he takes it on his own terms. The drifter takes whatever he can get, but he takes what he gets on my terms.

Stating the matter in another way, the non-drifter borrows money from a legitimate banker, if he wants it, and pays a legitimate rate of interest. The drifter goes to the pawn shop, hocks his watch, and pays a suicidal rate of interest for his loan.

Q So I draw from your claims the conclusion that your hand is mixed up somehow in all of people's troubles and miseries, even though your presence may not be visible?

A **My unwilling workers are often my best workers. You see, my unwilling workers are those whom I cannot control with**

some combination of bribes, people whom I have to master by fear or through some form of misfortune. They do not wish to serve me, but they cannot avoid it because they are eternally bound to me by the habit of drifting.

Q Now I am beginning to better understand your technique. You bribe your victims through their natural desires and lead them astray while you induce them to become drifters if they respond to your lure. If they refuse to respond, you plant the seed of fear in their minds or trap them through some form of misfortune, and hog-tie them while they are down. Is that your method?

A **That is exactly the way I work. Clever, don't you think?**

Q Which do you prefer to serve as your propagandists—the young or the old?

A **The young, of course! They can be influenced by most bribes more easily than people of mature judgment. Moreover, they have longer to remain in my service.**

Q Your Majesty has given me a clear description of drifting. Tell me what must be done to insure against the habit of drifting. I want a complete formula that anyone can use.

A **Protection against drifting lies within easy reach of every human being who has a normal body and a sound mind. The self-defense can be applied through these simple methods:**

1. **Do your own thinking on all occasions. The fact that human beings are given complete control over nothing save the power to think their own thoughts is laden with significance.**

2. Decide definitely what you want from life; then create a plan for attaining it and be willing to sacrifice everything else, if necessary, rather than accept permanent defeat.

3. Analyze temporary defeat, no matter of what nature or cause, and extract from it the seed of an equivalent advantage.

4. Be willing to render useful service equivalent to the value of all material things you demand of life, and render the service first.

5. Recognize that your brain is a receiving set that can be attuned to receive communications from the universal storehouse of Infinite Intelligence, to help you transmute your desires into their physical equivalent.

6. Recognize that your greatest asset is time, the only thing except the power of thought which you own outright, and the one thing which can be shaped into whatever material things you want. Budget your time so none of it is wasted.

7. Recognize the truth that fear generally is a filler with which the Devil occupies the unused portion of your mind. It is only a state of mind which you can control by filling the space it occupies with faith in your ability to make life provide you with whatever you demand of it.

8. When you pray, do not beg! Demand what you want and insist upon getting exactly that, with no substitutes.

9. Recognize that life is a cruel taskmaster and that either you master it or it masters you. There is no half-way or compromising point. Never accept from life anything you do not want. If that which you do not want is temporarily forced

upon you, you can refuse, in your own mind, to accept it and it will make way for the thing you do want.

10. Lastly, remember that your dominating thoughts attract, through a definite law of nature, by the shortest and most convenient route, their physical counterpart. Be careful what your thoughts dwell upon.

Q That list looks imposing. Give me a simple formula, combining all the ten points. If you had to combine all ten in one, what would it be?

A Be definite in everything you do and never leave unfinished thoughts in the mind. Form the habit of reaching definite decisions on all subjects.

Q Can the habit of drifting be broken, or does it become permanent once it has been formed?

A The habit can be broken if the victim has enough will power, providing it is done in time. There is a point beyond which the habit can never be broken. Beyond that point the victim is mine. He resembles a fly that has been caught in a spider's web. He may struggle, but he cannot get out. Each move he makes entangles him more securely. The web in which I entangle my victims permanently is a law of nature not yet isolated by, or understood by, men of science.

✦ *Chapter Six* ✦

HYPNOTIC RHYTHM

Q What is this mysterious law through which you take permanent control of people's bodies even before you take over their souls? The whole world will want to know more about this law and how it operates.

A **It will be hard to describe the law so you will understand it, but you may call it "hypnotic rhythm." It is the same law through which people can be hypnotized.**

Q So you have the power to use the laws of nature as a web in which you bind your victims in eternal control. Is that your claim?

A **That is not only my claim. It is the truth! I take over their minds and bodies even before they die whenever I can lure them or frighten them into hypnotic rhythm.**

Q What is hypnotic rhythm? How do you use it to gain permanent mastery over human beings?

A **I will have to go back into time and space and give you a brief elementary description of how nature uses hypnotic rhythm. Otherwise you will not be able to understand my description of how I use this universal law to control human beings.**

Q Go ahead, but keep your story confined to simple illustrations which come within the range of my own experience and knowledge of natural laws.

A **Very well, I shall do my best. You, of course, know that nature maintains a perfect balance between all the elements and all the energy in the universe. You can see that the stars and the planets move with perfect precision, each one keeping** its own place in time and space. You can see that the seasons of the year come and go with perfect regularity. You can see that an oak tree grows from an acorn and a pine grows from the seed of its ancestor. An acorn never produces a pine and a pine seed never produces an oak.

These are simple things which anyone can understand; what one cannot see is the universal law through which nature maintains perfect balance throughout the myriad of universes.

You earthbound caught a fragmentary glimpse of this great universal law when Newton discovered that it holds your earth in its position and causes all material objects to be attracted toward the center of the earth. He called the law gravitation.

But he did not go far enough in his study of the law. If he had, he would have discovered that the same law which holds your earth in position and helps nature to maintain a perfect balance over the four dimensions—in which all matter and energy are contained—is the web in which I entangle and control the minds of human beings.

Q Tell me more of this astounding law of hypnotic rhythm.

A As I have already stated, there is a universal form of energy with which nature keeps a perfect balance between all matter and energy. She makes specialized use of this universal building material by breaking it up into different wavelengths. The breaking-up process is carried on through habit.

You will better understand what I am trying to convey if I compare it with the method by which one learns to play music. At first the notes are memorized in the mind. Then they are related to one another through melody and rhythm. By repetition the melody and rhythm become fixed in the mind. Observe how relentlessly the musician must repeat a tune before he masters it. Through repetition the musical notes blend and then you have music.

Any impulse of thought that the mind repeats over and over through habit forms an organized rhythm. Undesirable habits can be broken. They must be broken before they assume the proportions of rhythm. Are you following me?

Q Yes.

A Well, to continue, rhythm is the last stage of habit! Any thought or physical movement which is repeated over and over through the principle of habit finally reaches the proportion of rhythm.

Then the habit cannot be broken because nature takes it over and makes it permanent. It is something like a whirlpool in water. An object may keep floating indefinitely unless it is caught in a whirlpool. Then it is carried round and round but it cannot escape. The energy with which people think may be compared with water in a river.

Q So this is the way in which you take control of the minds of people, is it?

A Yes. All I have to do to gain control over any mind is to induce its owner to drift.

Q Am I to understand that the habit of drifting is the major danger through which people lose their prerogative or privilege of thinking their own thoughts and shaping their own earthly destinations?

A That and much more. Drifting is also the habit through which I take over their souls after they give up their physical bodies.

Q Then the only way a human being can be saved from eternal annihilation is by maintaining control over his own mind while he is on this earth. Is that true?

A **You have stated the truth perfectly! Those who control and use their own minds escape my web. I get all the others as naturally as the sun sets in the west.**

Says the Devil: *"Those who control and use their own minds escape my web."*

Q Is that all there is to the business of being saved from eternal annihilation? Doesn't what you call your opposition have anything to do with saving people?

A **I can see that you do think very deeply. My opposition—the power you earthbound call God—has everything to do with the salvation of people from eternal annihilation, and for that reason it is my opposition who provides every human being with the privilege of using his own mind.**

If you use that power by maintaining control over your own mind, you become a part of it when you give up your physical body. If you neglect to use it, then I have the privilege of taking advantage of the neglect through the law of hypnotic rhythm.

Q How much of a person do you take over when you gain control of him?

A **Everything that is left after he ceases to control and use his own mind.**

Q In other words, when you gain control of a person you take over all there is of his individuality up to the time that he quits using his own mind? Is that correct?

A **That is how I operate.**

Q What do you do with people whom you control before death? Of what good are they to you while they live?

A **I use them, or what is left of than after I take charge, as propagandists to help me prepare the minds of others to drift.**

Q You not only fool people into destroying their power to control their own minds, but you use them to help you trap others?

A **Yes, I let no opportunity get away from me.**

Q Let us come back to the subject of hypnotic rhythm. Tell me more of how this law works. Show me how you use individuals to help you gain control over others. I want to know something of the most effective way you use hypnotic rhythm.

A **Oh, that is easy! The thing I like best is to fill the minds of people with fear. Once I fill one's mind with fear I have little trouble causing him to drift until I have entangled him in the web of hypnotic rhythm.**

Q What human fear best serves your purpose?

A **The fear of death.**

Q Why is the fear of death your favorite weapon?

A Because no one knows, and by the very nature of the laws of the universe, no one can prove definitely what happens after death. This uncertainty frightens people out of their wits.

People who give over their minds to fear—any sort of fear—neglect to use their minds and begin to drift. Eventually they drift into the whirlpool of hypnotic rhythm from which they may never escape.

Q Then you do not mind what religious leaders think or say of you when they speak of death?

A Not as long as they say something! If the churches should stop talking about me, my cause would receive a severe setback. Every attack made against me fixes the fear of me in the minds of all who are influenced by it. You see, opposition is the thing that keeps some people from drifting! Providing they do not yield to it.

Q Since you claim the churches help instead of hindering your cause, tell me what would give you cause to worry?

A My only worry is that someday a real thinker may appear on earth.

Q What would happen if a thinker did appear?

A You ask me what would happen? I'll tell you what would happen. People would learn the greatest of all truths—that the time they spend in fearing something would, if reversed, give them all they want in the material world and save them from me after death. Isn't that worth thinking about?

> **Says the Devil:** ***"The time they [people] spend in fearing something would, if reversed, give them all they want in the material world and save them from me after death."***

Q What is keeping such a thinker from appearing in the world?

A Fear of criticism! It may interest you to know that the fear of criticism is the only effective weapon I have with which to whip you. If you were not afraid to publish this confession after you wring it from me, I would lose my earthly kingdom.

Q And if I did surprise you and publish it, how long would it be until you lost your kingdom?

A Just long enough for one generation of children to grow into understanding. You cannot take the adults from me. I have them too securely sewed up. But if you published this confession, it would be sufficient to keep me from gaining control of the yet unborn and those who have not yet reached the age of reason. You wouldn't dare publish what I have told you about the religious leaders. They would crucify you!

Q I thought the savage practice of crucifixion went out of style two thousand years ago.

A I don't mean crucifixion on a cross. I mean social and financial crucifixion. Your income would be shut off. You would become a social outcast. Religious leaders and their followers alike would treat you with scorn.

Q Suppose I should choose to throw in my lot with the select few who make a pretense of using their own minds rather than fear the masses who do not—the masses of whom you claim 98 percent?

A If you have courage enough to do this, you will crimp my style.

A chill ran down my spine when I first read this . . . since circumstances did indeed prevent this manuscript, written in 1938, from being published until now, well after Hill's death in 1970. Was the delayed publication of the work truly caused by his wife's "fear of criticism" and concern over the reaction of religious leaders and public school advocates . . . or was it due to the work of the Devil himself? And now, the family and the Foundation have decided it is time to share the manuscript with the world. Shall we heed Hill's wisdom, discover our "other selves," and take control of our own minds, reclaiming our destiny?

Q Why do you lay claim to no scientist? Don't you like scientists?

A Oh yes, I like all people well enough, but true scientists are out of my reach.

Q Why?

A Because they think for themselves and spend their time studying natural laws. They deal with cause and effect. They deal with facts wherever they find them. But do not make the mistake of believing scientists have no religion. They have a very definite religion.

Q What is their religion?

A **The religion of truth! The religion of natural law! If the world ever produces an accurate thinker with ability to fathom the deeply buried secret of life and death, you can be sure that science will be responsible for the catastrophe.**

Q Catastrophe to whom?

A **To me, of course!**

Q Let's get back to the subject of hypnotic rhythm. I want to know more about it. Is it something like the principle through which people can hypnotize one another?

A **It is precisely the same thing. I have already told you so. Why do you repeat your questions?**

Q That is an old worldly custom of mine, Your Majesty. For your enlightenment I will tell you I am forcing you to repeat many of your statements for the sake of emphasis. I am also trying to see if I can catch you in a lie! Don't dodge the issue. Get back to hypnotic rhythm and tell me all you know about it. Am I a victim of it?

A **Not now, but you barely missed falling into my web. You drifted toward the whirlpool of hypnotic rhythm, until you discovered how to force me into making this confession. Then I lost control of you!**

Q How interesting. You are not trying to recapture me through flattery, are you?

A That would be the best bribe I could offer you. It is the bribe I used on you effectively before you got the upper hand of me.

Q With what did you flatter me?

A With many things, chief among them sex and the desire for self-expression.

Q What effect did your bribes have on me?

A They caused you to neglect your major purpose in life and started you to drifting.

Q Was that all you did to me through your bribes?

A That was plenty.

Q But I am back on the track and out of your reach now, am I not?

A Yes, you are temporarily out of my reach because you are not drifting.

Q What broke your spell over me and released me from the habit of drifting?

A My answer may humiliate you. Do you want to hear it?

Q Go ahead and give it to me, Your Majesty. I wish to learn how much truth I can stand.

A When you found a great love in the woman of your choice, I lost my grip on you.

Q So you are going to accuse me of hiding behind a woman's skirts, are you?

A **No, not hiding. I wouldn't put it that way. I would say you have learned how to give yourself a solid background with the embellishment of a woman's mind.**

Q The woman's skirt has nothing to do with it then?

A **No, but her brain does. When you and your wife began to combine your two brains, through your habit of "Master Minding" every day, you stumbled upon the secret power with which you forced me into this confession.**

Q Is that the truth, or are you trying to flatter me again?

A **I could flatter you if I had you alone, but I cannot flatter you while you have the use of your wife's mind.**

Q I am beginning to catch on to something important. I am beginning to understand what was meant by the writer of that passage in the Bible which says substantially, "When two or more meet together and ask for anything in My name, it shall be granted." It is true, then, that two minds are better than one.

A **It is not only true, it is necessary before anyone can continuously contact the great storehouse of Infinite Intelligence wherein is stored all that is, all that ever was, and all that can ever be.**

Q Is there such a storehouse?

A **If there had not been, you would not—could not—now be humiliating me with this silly forced confession.**

Q Isn't it dangerous to give this sort of information to the world?

A **Sure, it is dangerous to me. If I were you, I would not give it out.**

Q Let us get back, now, to the technique through which you fasten on your victims the habit of drifting. What is the very first step a drifter must take to break the habit?

A **A burning desire to break it! You of course know that no one can be hypnotized by another person without his willingness to be hypnotized. The willingness may assume the form of indifference toward life generally, lack of ambition, fear, lack of definiteness of purpose, and many other forms. Nature does not need one's consent in order to place him under the spell of hypnotic rhythm. It needs only to find him off guard, through any form of neglect to use his own mind. Remember this: whatever you have, you use it or you lose it!**

All successful attempts to break the habit of drifting must be done before nature makes the habit permanent, through hypnotic rhythm.

Q As I understand you, hypnotic rhythm is a natural law through which nature fixes the vibration of all environments. Is that true?

A **Yes, nature uses hypnotic rhythm to make one's dominating thoughts and one's thought-habits permanent. That is why poverty is disease. Nature makes it so by fixing permanently the thought-habits of all who accept poverty as an unavoidable circumstance.**

Through this same law of hypnotic rhythm, nature will also fix permanently positive thoughts of opulence and prosperity.

Perhaps you will better understand the working principle of hypnotic rhythm if I tell you its nature is to fix permanently all habits whether they are mental or physical. If your mind fears poverty, your mind will attract poverty. If your mind demands opulence and expects it, your mind will attract the physical and financial equivalents of opulence. This is in accordance with an immutable law of nature.

Hill first wrote about the Law of Attraction in the March 1919 issue of his *Golden Rule* magazine. Within the last decade, this immutable law of nature has been popularized around the world by the resounding success of the book and movie *The Secret*.

Q Did the writer of that sentence in the Bible, "Whatsoever a man soweth, that shall he also reap," have in mind this law of nature?

A He could have nothing else in mind. The statement is true. You can see evidence of its truth in all human relationships.

Q And that is why the man who forms the habit of drifting through life must accept whatever life hands him. Is that correct?

A That is absolutely correct. Life pays the drifter its own price, on its own terms. The non-drifter makes life pay on his own terms.

Q Doesn't the question of morals enter into what one gets from life?

A To be sure, but only for the reason that one's morals have an influence on one's thoughts. No one can collect what he wants from life merely by being good, if that is what you want to know.

Q No, I guess not. I see what you mean. We are all where we are and what we are because of our own deeds.

A No, not exactly. You are where you are and what you are because of your thoughts and your deeds.

Q Then there is no such reality as luck, is there?

A Emphatically no. Circumstances which people do not understand are classified under the heading of luck. Back of every reality is a cause. Often the cause is so far removed from the effect that the circumstance can be explained only by attributing it to the operation of luck. Nature knows no such law as luck. It is a man-made hypothesis with which he explains away things he does not understand. The terms "luck" and "miracle" are twin sisters. Neither of them has any real existence except in the imaginations of people. Both are used to explain that which people do not understand. Remember this: everything having a real existence is capable of proof. Keep this one truth in mind and you will become a sounder thinker.

Q Which is more important, one's thoughts or one's deeds?

A **All deeds follow thoughts. There can be no deeds without their having first been patterned in thought. Moreover, all thoughts have a tendency to clothe themselves in their physical counterpart. One's dominating thoughts, that is, the thoughts one mixes with the emotions, desire, hope, faith, fear, hate, greed, enthusiasm, not only have a tendency to clothe themselves in their physical equivalent, but they are bound to do so.**

Q That reminds me to ask you to tell me more about yourself. Where, in addition to the minds of people, do you dwell and operate?

A **I operate wherever there is something I can control and appropriate. I have already told you I am the negative portion of the electron of matter.**

- **I am the explosion in lightning.**
- **I am the pain in disease and physical suffering.**
- **I am the unseen general in warfare.**
- **I am the unknown commissioner of poverty and famine.**
- **I am the executioner extraordinaire at death.**
- **I am the inspirer of lust after the flesh.**
- **I am the creator of jealousy and envy and greed.**
- **I am the instigator of fear.**
- **I am the genius who converts the achievements of men of science into instruments of death.**

- I am the destroyer of harmony in all manner of human relationships.
- I am the antithesis of justice.
- I am the driving force in all immorality.
- I am the stalemate of all good.
- I am anxiety, suspense, superstition, and insanity.
- I am the destroyer of hope and faith.
- I am the inspirer of destructive gossip and scandal.
- I am the discourager of free and independent thought.
- In brief, I am the creator of all forms of human misery, the instigator of discouragement and disappointment.

Q And you do not call that cold and cruel?

A I call that definite and dependable.

The world depression broke up the habits of men everywhere and redistributed the sources of opportunity in all walks of life on an unprecedented scale.

The drifter's pet alibi, with which he tries to explain away his undesirable position, is his cry that the world has run dry of opportunities.

Non-drifters do not wait for opportunity to be placed in their way. They create opportunity to fit their desires and demands of life!

Hill speaks of the great opportunities that arose during the Great Depression and the fortunes that were made by those who seized those opportunities. I believe that Hill would say the same thing in our own day . . . many opportunities exist today because of the economic turmoil. Will you seize one and create your own opportunity to fit your desires and demands of life?

Q Are non-drifters smart enough to avoid the influence of hypnotic rhythm?

A No one is smart enough to dodge the influence of hypnotic rhythm. One could just as easily avoid the influence of the law of gravity. The law of hypnotic rhythm fixes permanently the dominating thoughts of men, whether they be drifters or non-drifters.

There is no reason why a non-drifter would want to avoid the influence of hypnotic rhythm, because that law is favorable to him. It helps him convert his dominating aims, plans, and purposes into their physical replicas. It fixes his habits of thought and makes them permanent.

Only the drifter would wish to dodge the influence of hypnotic rhythm.

Q For the better portion of my adult life I have been a drifter. How did I manage to escape being swept into the whirlpool of hypnotic rhythm?

A You haven't escaped. The major portion of your dominating thoughts and desires, since you reached adulthood, has been a well-defined, definite desire to understand all the potentialities of the mind.

You may have drifted on thoughts of lesser importance, but you did not drift in connection with this desire. Because you did not drift, you are now recording a document which gives you exactly what your dominating thoughts demanded of life.

Q Why doesn't your opposition use hypnotic rhythm to make permanent one's higher thoughts and nobler deeds? Why does your opposition permit you to use this stupendous force as a means of entangling people in a web of evil spun by their own thoughts and deeds? Why does your opposition not outwit you by binding people with thoughts which build and lift them above your influence?

A The law of hypnotic rhythm is available to all who will use it. I make use of it more effectively than does my opposition because I offer people more attractive bribes to think my sort of thoughts and indulge in my sort of deeds.

Q In other words, you control people by making negative thinking and destructive deeds pleasing to them. Is that correct?

A That is the idea, exactly!

✦ *Chapter Seven* ✦

SEEDS OF FEAR

Q I HAVE OFTEN WONDERED WHY your opposition—what we earthbound call God—does not annihilate you? Can you tell me why?

A Because the power is as much mine as his. It is as available to me as to him. That is what I have been trying to get over to you. The highest power in the universe can be used for constructive purposes, through what you call God, or it can be used for negative purposes, through what you call the Devil. And something more important still, it can be used by any human being just as effectively as by God or the Devil.

Q You make a far-reaching claim. Can you prove your claim?

A Yes, but it would be better if you proved it for yourself. The Devil's word is not worth much among you earthbound sinners. Neither is God's word. You fear the Devil and refuse to trust your God; therefore you have but one source available through which you may appropriate the benefit of universal power, and that is by trusting and using your own power of thought. This is the direct road to the universal storehouse of Infinite Intelligence. There is no other road available to any human being.

Q Why have we earthbound not found the road to Infinite Intelligence sooner?

A Because I have intercepted you and led you off the path by planting in your minds thoughts which destroy your power to use your minds constructively. I have made it attractive to you to use the Power of Infinite Intelligence to attain negative ends, through greed, avarice, lust, envy, and hatred. Remember, your mind attracts that which your mind dwells upon. To divert you away from my opposition, I had only to feed you on thoughts helpful to my cause.

Q If I understand what you are saying, you are admitting that no human being need fear the Devil or worry about how to flatter God!

A That is it precisely. This admission may put a crimp in my style, but I have this satisfaction of knowing it may also slow down my opposition by sending people direct to the source of all power.

Here, as in some other points during the dialogue, Hill gets explicitly theological. Using the Devil as a foil and letting words come out of the mouth of the symbol of evil, Napoleon Hill can lay out his thoughts and feelings about God—Infinite Intelligence—as the ultimate source for his overall philosophy of success.

Q In other words, if you cannot control people through negative bribes or fear, then you wish to kick over the entire apple cart and show people how to go directly to God? Are you, by any chance, in politics too? Your technique seems frightfully familiar.

A Am I in politics? If I am not in politics, who do you believe starts depressions and forces people into wars? Surely you would not lay this at the door of my opposition? As I have already told you, I have allies in all walks of life, to help me in connection with all human relationships.

Q Why don't you take over the churches and use them outright in your cause?

A **Do you think I am a fool? Who would keep alive the fear of the Devil if I subdued the churches? Who would serve as a decoy to attract the attention of people while I manipulate their minds if I did not have some agency through which to sow the seeds of fear and doubt? The cleverest thing I do is to use the allies of my opposition to keep the fear of hell burning in the minds of people. As long as people fear something, no matter what, I will keep a grip on them.**

Q I am beginning to see your scheme. You use the churches to plant the seed of fear and uncertainty and indefiniteness in the minds of people. These negative states of mind cause people to form the habit of drifting. This habit crystallizes into permanency through the law of hypnotic rhythm; then the victim is helpless to help himself, is that right? Hypnotic rhythm, then, is something to be watched and respected?

A **A better way of stating the truth is that hypnotic rhythm is something to be studied, understood, and voluntarily applied to attain definite desired ends.**

Q If the force of hypnotic rhythm is not voluntarily applied to attain definite ends, may it be a great danger?

A **Yes, and for the reason that it operates automatically. If it is not consciously applied to attain a desired end, it can, and it will, operate to attain undesired ends.**

Take the simple illustration of climate, for example. Anyone can see and understand that nature forces every living thing and every element of matter to adjust itself to her

climates. In the tropics she creates trees which bear fruit and reproduce themselves. She forces the trees to adjust themselves to her scorching sun! She forces them to put out leaves suitable for protection against the rays of the sun. These same trees could not survive if removed to the arctic regions where nature has established an entirely different climate.

In the colder climate she creates trees which are adjusted to survive and to reproduce themselves, but they could not survive if transplanted in the tropical regions. In the same manner, nature clothes her animals, giving to those in each different climate a covering suited to their comfort and survival in that climate.

In a similar manner, nature forces upon the minds of men the influences of their environment, which are stronger than the individual's own thoughts. Children are forced to take on the nature of all influences of those around them unless their own thoughts are stronger than the influences.

Nature sets up a definite rhythm for every environment, and everything within the range of that rhythm is forced to conform to it. Man, alone, has the power to establish his own rhythm of thought providing he exercises this privilege before hypnotic rhythm has forced upon him the influences of his environment.

Every home, every place of business, every town and village and every street and community center has its own definite, discernible rhythm. If you wish to know what a difference there is in the rhythms of streets, take a walk up Fifth Avenue, in New York, and then down a street in the slums! All forms of rhythm become permanent with time.

Q Does each individual have his own rhythm of thought?

A Yes. That is precisely the major difference between individuals. The person who thinks in terms of power, success, opulence, sets up a rhythm which attracts these desirable possessions. The person who thinks in terms of misery, failure, defeat, discouragement, and poverty attracts these undesirable influences. This explains why both success and failure are the result of habit. Habit establishes one's rhythm of thought, and that rhythm attracts the object of one's dominating thoughts.

Q Hypnotic rhythm is something resembling a magnet which attracts things for which it has a magnetic affinity. Is that correct?

A Yes, that is correct. That is why the poverty-stricken herd themselves into the same communities. It explains that old saying, "Misery loves company." It also explains why people who begin to succeed in any undertaking find that success multiplies, with less effort, as time goes on.

All successful people use hypnotic rhythm, either consciously or unconsciously, by expecting and demanding success. The demand becomes a habit, hypnotic rhythm takes over the habit, and the law of harmonious attraction translates it into its physical equivalent.

Q In other words, if I know what I want from life, demand it and back my demand by a willingness to pay life's price for what I want, and refuse to accept any substitutes, the law of hypnotic rhythm takes over my desire and helps, by natural and logical means, to transmute it into its physical counterpart. Is that true?

A That describes the way the law works.

Q Science has established irrefutable evidence that people are what they are because of heredity and environment. They bring over with them at birth a combination of all the physical qualities of all their numberless ancestors. After they arrive here, they reach the age of self-consciousness and from there on they shape their own personalities and more or less fix their own earthly destinations as the result of the environmental influences to which they are subjected, especially the influences which control them during early childhood. These two facts have been so well established there is no room for any intelligent person to question them. How can hypnotic rhythm change the nature of a physical body which is a combination of thousands of ancestors who have lived and died before one is born? How can hypnotic rhythm change the influence of one's environment? People who are born in poverty and ignorance have a strong tendency to remain poverty-stricken and ignorant all through life. What, if anything, can hypnotic rhythm do about this?

A **Hypnotic rhythm cannot change the nature of the physical body one inherits at birth, but it can and it does modify, change, control, and make permanent one's environmental influences.**

Q If I understand what you mean, a human being is forced by nature to take on and become a part of the environment he chooses or the environment that may be forced upon him?

A **That is correct, but there are ways and means by which an individual may resist the influences of an environment he does not wish to accept, and also a method of procedure by which one may reverse the application of hypnotic rhythm from negative to positive ends.**

Q Do you mean that there is a definite method by which hypnotic rhythm can be made to serve instead of destroy one?

A **I mean just that.**

Q Tell me how this astounding end may be attained.

A **For my description to be of any practical value, it will be necessarily lengthy because it will have to cover seven principles of psychology which must be understood and applied by all who use hypnotic rhythm to aid them in forcing life to yield that which they want.**

Q Then break your description into seven parts, each giving a detailed analysis of one of the seven principles, with simple instructions for its practical application.

I have always been fascinated with how Hill's mind works. After building a case for impending doom, he now reveals the lifeline for anyone seeking success. This is a critical turning point. As you read further, will his "seven principles" capture your imagination, as they did mine?

✦ Chapter Eight ✦

DEFINITENESS OF PURPOSE

Q YOUR MAJESTY WILL NOW PROCEED to unfold the secrets of the seven principles through which human beings may force life to provide them with spiritual, mental, and physical freedom.

In the rest of the book, Hill discusses these seven principles to attain spiritual, mental, and physical freedom:

1. **Definiteness of purpose**
2. **Mastery over self**
3. **Learning from adversity**
4. **Controlling environmental influence (associations)**
5. **Time (giving permanency to positive, rather than negative thought-habits and developing wisdom)**
6. **Harmony (acting with definiteness of purpose to become the dominating influence in your own mental, spiritual, and physical environment)**
7. **Caution (thinking through your plan before you act)**

Do not be sparing in your description of these principles. I want a complete illustration of how the principles may be used by anyone who chooses to use them. Tell us all you know about the principle of *definiteness of purpose*.

The interrogator gains some momentum here and goes for the jugular. Do we have the courage, at moments of opportunity, to act as aggressively and with definiteness of purpose?

A If you go through with this mad idea of publishing my confession, you will open the gates of hell and turn loose all the precious souls I have collected back down through the ages. You will deprive me of souls yet unborn. You will release from my bondage millions now living. Stop, I beg of you.

Q Open up. Let's hear what you have to say about the principle of definiteness of purpose.

A You are pouring water on the fires of hell, but the responsibility is yours, not mine. I may as well tell you that any human being who can be definite in his aims and plans can make life hand over whatever is wanted.

Q That is a broad claim, Your Majesty. Do you wish to tone it down a bit?

A Tone it down? No, I wish to tone it up. When you hear what I now have to say, you will understand why the principle of definiteness is so important. My opposition uses a clever little trick to cheat me of my control over people. The opposition knows that definiteness of purpose closes the door of one's mind so tightly against me that I cannot break through unless I can induce one to form the habit of drifting.

Q Why doesn't your opposition give your secret to all people by telling them to avoid you through definiteness of purpose? You have already admitted that two out of every hundred people belong to your opposition.

A Because I am more clever than my opposition. I draw people away from definiteness with my promises. You see, I control more people than my opposition because I am a

better salesman and a better showman. I attract people by feeding them liberally of the thought-habits in which they like to indulge.

Q Is definiteness of purpose something with which one must be born or may it be acquired?

A **Everyone, as I have told you before, is born with the privilege of being definite, but 98 out of every 100 people lose this privilege by sleeping on it. The privilege of definiteness can be maintained only by adopting it as a policy by which one is guided in all the affairs of life.**

Q Oh, I see! One takes advantage of the principle of definiteness just as one may build a strong physical body—through constant, systematic use. Is that it?

A **You have stated the truth clearly and accurately.**

Q Now I think we are getting somewhere, Your Majesty. We have at long last found the starting point from which all who become self-determining in life must take off.

We have discovered, from your astounding confession, that your greatest asset is man's lack of caution, which enables you to lead him into the jungle of indefiniteness through simple bribes.

We have learned, beyond the question of doubt, that anyone who adopts definiteness of purpose as a policy and uses it in all of his daily experiences cannot be induced to form the habit of drifting. Without the aid of the drifting habit you are powerless to attract people through promises. Is this correct?

A **I couldn't have stated the truth more clearly myself.**

Q Go ahead, now, and describe how people neglect their privilege of being free and self-determining through indefiniteness and drifting.

A I have already made brief reference to this principle, but I will now go into more minute details as to how the principle works.

I shall have to begin at the time of birth. When a child is born, it brings with it nothing but a physical body representing the evolutionary results of millions of years of ancestry.

Its mind is a total blank. When the child reaches the age of consciousness and begins to recognize the objects of its surroundings, it begins, also, to imitate others.

Imitation becomes a fixed habit. Naturally the child imitates, first of all, its parents! Then it begins to imitate its other relatives and daily associates, including its religious instructors and schoolteachers.

The imitation extends not merely to physical expression, but also to thought expression. If a child's parents fear me and express that fear within range of the child's hearing, the child picks up the fear through the habit of imitation and stores it away as a part of its subconscious stock of beliefs.

If the child's religious instructor expresses any form of fear of me (and they all do, in one form or another), that fear is added to the similar fear passed to the child by its parents, and the two forms of negative limitation are stored away in the subconscious mind to be drawn upon and used by me later in life.

In a similar way the child learns, by imitation, to limit its power of thought by filling its mind with envy, hatred, greed, lust, revenge, and all the other negative impulses of thought which destroy all possibility of definiteness.

Meanwhile I move in and induce the child to drift until I bind its mind through hypnotic rhythm.

Q Am I to understand from your remarks that you have to gain control of people while they are very young or lose your opportunity at them altogether?

A I prefer to claim them before they come into possession of their own minds. Once any person learns the power of his own thoughts, he becomes positive and difficult to subdue. As a matter of fact, I cannot control any human being who discovers and uses the principle of definiteness.

Q Is the habit of definiteness a permanent protection against your control?

A No, not by any means. Definiteness closes the door of one's mind to me only as long as that person follows the principle as a matter of policy. Once any person hesitates, procrastinates, or becomes indefinite about anything, he is just one step removed from my control.

Says the Devil: *"Once any person hesitates, procrastinates, or becomes indefinite about anything, he is just one step removed from my control."*

✦ ✦ ✦ ✦ ✦ ✦ ✦ ✦ ✦ ✦

The metaphysical and spiritual aspects of the author's philosophy are on display in these responses by the Devil. What he calls "definiteness" is today often called "intention" or being "goal-driven" or "purpose-driven."

Q What has definiteness to do with one's material circumstances? I want to know if one may acquire power through definiteness of purpose without inviting destruction through the law of compensation.

A **Your question limits my illustrations because there are so few people in the world who understand, and there have been so few in the past who understood, how to use definiteness of purpose without attracting to themselves the negative application of the law of compensation.**

Here you are forcing me to disclose one of my most prized tricks. I am bound to tell you that I eventually reclaim for my cause all who escape me temporarily through definiteness of purpose. The reclamation is made by filling the mind with greed for power and the love of egotistical expression, until the individual falls into the habit of violating the rights of others. Then I step in with the law of compensation and reclaim my victim.

Q So I see from your admission that definiteness of purpose may be dangerous in proportion to its possibility as a power. Is that true?

A **Yes, and what is more important, every principle of good carries with it the seed of an equivalent danger.**

Q That is hard to believe. What danger, for example, can there be in the habit of love of truth?

A **The danger lies in the word "habit." All habits, save only that of the love of definiteness of purpose, may lead to the habit of drifting. Love for truth, unless it assumes the proportion of definite pursuit of truth, may become similar to all other good intentions. You know, of course, what I do with good intentions.**

"All habits, save only that of the love of definiteness of purpose, may lead to the habit of drifting."

Q Is love for one's relatives also dangerous?

A The love for anything or anyone, save only the love of definiteness of purpose, may become dangerous. Love is a state of mind which beclouds reason, saps will power, and blinds one to facts and truth.

Everyone who becomes self-determining and gains spiritual freedom to think his own thoughts must examine carefully every emotion that seems even remotely related to love.

You may be surprised to know that love is one of my most effective baits. With it I lead into the habit of drifting those whom I could attract with nothing else.

That is why I have placed it at the head of my list of bribes. Show me what any person loves most and I will have my cue as to how that person can be induced to drift until I bind him with hypnotic rhythm.

Love and fear, combined, give me the most effective weapons with which I induce people to drift. One is as helpful to me as the other. Both have the effect of causing people to neglect to develop definiteness in the use of their own minds. Give me control over a person's fears and tell me what he loves most and you may as well mark that person down as my slave. Both love and fear are emotional forces of such stupendous potency that either may completely set aside the power of will and the power of reason. Without will and reason there is nothing left to support definiteness of purpose.

Q But, Your Majesty, life would not be worth living if people never felt the emotion of love.

A **Ah! You are right as far as your reasoning goes, but you neglected to add that love should be under one's definite control at all times.**

Of course, love is a desirable state of mind, but it also is a palliative which may be used to limit or destroy reason and will power, both of which rate above love in importance to human beings who want freedom and self-determination.

Q I understand from what you say that people who gain power must harden their emotions, master fear, and subdue love. Is that correct?

A **People who gain and maintain power must become definite in all their thoughts and all their deeds. If that is what you call hard, then they must become hard.**

Q Let us look into the sources of advantage of definiteness in the everyday affairs of life. Which is more apt to succeed, a weak plan applied with definiteness, or a sound strong plan indefinitely applied?

A **Weak plans have a way of becoming strong if definitely applied.**

Q You mean that any plan definitely put into continuous action in pursuit of a definite purpose may be successful even if it is not the best plan?

A **Yes, I mean just that. Definiteness of purpose plus definiteness of plan by which the purpose is to be achieved generally succeeds, no matter how weak the plan may be. The major** difference between a sound and an unsound plan is that the sound plan, if definitely applied, may be carried out more quickly than an unsound plan.

Q In other words, if one cannot be always right one can and should be always definite? Is that what you are trying to get across to me?

A That is the idea. People who are definite in both their plans and their purposes never accept temporary defeat as being more than an urge to greater effort. You can see for yourself that this sort of policy is bound to win if it is followed with definiteness.

Q Can a person who moves with definiteness of both plan and purpose be always sure of success?

A No. The best of plans sometimes misfire, but the person who moves with definiteness recognizes the difference between temporary defeat and failure. When plans fail he substitutes others but he does not change his purpose. He perseveres. Eventually he finds a plan that succeeds.

"The person who moves with definiteness recognizes the difference between temporary defeat and failure. When plans fail he substitutes others but he does not change his purpose. He perseveres."

Q Will a plan based upon immoral or unjust ends succeed as quickly as one motivated by a keen sense of justice and morality?

A Through the operation of the law of compensation, everyone reaps that which he sows. Plans based on unjust or immoral motives may bring temporary success, but enduring success must take into consideration the fourth dimension, time.

Time is the enemy of immorality and injustice. It is the friend of justice and morality. Failure to recognize this fact has been responsible for the crime wave among the youths of the world.

The youthful, inexperienced mind is apt to mistake temporary success for permanency. The youth often makes the mistake of coveting the temporary gains of immoral, unjust plans, but neglects to look ahead and observe the penalties which follow as definitely as night follows day.

Chapter Nine

EDUCATION AND RELIGION

Q THIS IS PRETTY DEEP STUFF, Your Majesty. Let us get back to the discussion of lighter and more concrete subjects that are likely to interest the majority of people. I am interested in discussing the things that make people happy and miserable, rich and poor, sick and healthy. In brief, I am interested in everything that can be used by human beings to make life pay satisfactory dividends in return for the effort that one puts into the business of living.

A **Very well, let us be definite.**

Q You have my idea. Your Majesty has a tendency to stray off into abstract details which most people can neither understand nor use in the solution of their problems. Could that, by any chance, be a definite plan of yours to answer my questions with indefinite answers? If that is your plan, it is a slick trick but it will not work. Go ahead now and tell me something more of the miseries and failures of human beings growing directly out of indefiniteness.

A **Why not permit me to tell you more of the pleasures and successes of people who understand and apply the principle of definiteness?**

Q I observe that sometimes people with definiteness of plan and purpose get what they ask from life only to find after they get it that they do not want it. What then?

A **Generally one can get rid of whatever is not wanted by application of the same principle of definiteness with which the thing was acquired. A life that is lived with fullness of peace of mind, contentment, and happiness always divests itself of everything it does not want. Anyone who submits to annoyance by things he does not want is not definite. He is a drifter.**

"A life that is lived with fullness of peace of mind, contentment, and happiness always divests itself of everything it does not want."

✦ ✦ ✦ ✦ ✦ ✦ ✦ ✦ ✦ ✦

How many of us are truly content? In a world where so many people are trying to "keep up with the Joneses," could we not all learn something here? Is there something in your life that you need to divest yourself of? Make a commitment to catch yourself when you are feeling annoyed . . . and remember the Devil's words, "Anyone who submits to annoyance by things he does not want is not definite. He is a drifter."

Q What about married people who cease to want each other? Should they separate, or is it true that all marriages are made in heaven and the contracting parties are, therefore, forever bound by their bargain, even though it may prove to be a poor one for both.

A First, let me correct that old saying that all marriages are made in heaven. I know of some which were made on my side of the fence. Minds which do not harmonize should never be forced to remain together in marriage or any other relationship. Friction and all forms of discord between minds lead inevitably to the habit of drifting, and of course to indefiniteness.

Q Aren't people sometimes bound to others by a relationship of duty which renders it impractical for them to take from life what they want most?

A "Duty" is one of the most abused and misunderstood words in existence. The first duty of every human being is to himself. Every person owes himself the duty of finding how to live a full and happy life. Beyond this, if one has time and energy not needed in the fulfillment of his own desires, one may assume responsibility for helping others.

"The first duty of every human being is to himself. Every person owes himself the duty of finding how to live a full and happy life."

✦ ✦ ✦ ✦ ✦ ✦ ✦ ✦ ✦ ✦

Of course, though compelled to answer accurately, the Devil still responds from the perspective of the Devil. Is it possible that Mother Teresa or Gandhi had a very different opinion on this issue? They lived their lives in service of others. How do you feel? Do you put finding a full and happy life first in your life? Do you agree with those who would argue that to truly be of service to others you need to take care of yourself first? Is it then possible that Mother Teresa and Gandhi found their full and happy lives—through service to others?

Q Isn't that a selfish attitude, and isn't selfishness one of the causes of failure to find happiness?

A I stand by my statement that there is no higher duty than that which one owes himself.

Q Doesn't a child owe something in the way of duty to its

parents who gave it life and sustenance during its periods of helplessness?

A Not at all. It is just the other way around. Parents owe their children everything they can give them in the way of knowledge. Beyond that, parents often spoil instead of helping their offspring by a false sense of duty which prompts them to indulge their children instead of forcing them to seek and gain knowledge at first hand.

Q I see what you mean. Your theory is that too much help thrust upon the youth encourages him to drift and become indefinite in all things. You believe that necessity is a teacher of great sagacity, that defeat carries with it an equivalent virtue, that unearned gifts of every nature may become a curse instead of a blessing. Is that correct?

Hill notes, *"Unearned gifts of every nature may become a curse instead of a blessing."* In our effort to give to our children, are we really cursing them? A very sobering thought, but also great advice, for parents.

A You have stated my philosophy perfectly. My belief is not theory. It is fact.

Q Then you do not advocate prayer as a means of gaining desirable ends?

A On the contrary I do advocate prayer, but not the sort of prayer that consists of empty, begging, meaningless words.

The sort of prayer against which I am helpless is the prayer of definiteness of purpose.

Q I never thought of definiteness of purpose as being a prayer. How can it be?

A Definiteness is in effect the only sort of prayer upon which one can rely. It places one in the way of using hypnotic rhythm to attain definite ends . . . by the mere act of appropriating it from the great universal storehouse of Infinite Intelligence. The appropriation, in case you are interested, takes place through definiteness of purpose, persistently pursued!

Q Why do the majority of prayers fail?

A They don't. All prayers bring that for which one prays.

Q But you just said that definiteness of purpose is the only sort of prayer upon which one can rely. Now you say that all prayers bring results. What do you mean?

A There is nothing inconsistent about it. The majority of people who pray go to prayer only after everything else fails them. Naturally they go with their minds filled with fear that the prayers will not be answered. Well, their fears are realized.

The person who goes to prayer with definiteness of purpose and faith in the attainment of that purpose puts into motion the laws of nature which transmute one's dominating desires into their physical equivalent. That is all there is to prayer.

One form of prayer is negative and brings only negative results. One form is positive and brings definite, positive results. Could anything be more simple?

People who whine and beg God to assume responsibility

for all their troubles and provide them with all the necessities and luxuries of life are too lazy to create what they want and translate it into existence through the power of their own minds.

When you hear a person praying for something that he should procure through his own efforts, you may be sure you are listening to a drifter. Infinite Intelligence favors only those who understand and adapt themselves to her laws. She makes no discrimination because of fine character or pleasing personality. These things help people negotiate their way through life more harmoniously with one another, but the source from which prayer is answered is not impressed by fine feathers. Nature's law is, "Know what you want, adapt yourself to my laws, and you shall have it."

The preceding question and answer push the boundaries of Hill's critique of organized religion versus personal spirituality and responsibility.

Q Does that harmonize with the teachings of Christ?

A Perfectly. Also it harmonizes with the teachings of all truly great philosophers.

Q Is your theory of definiteness in harmony with the philosophy of men of science?

A Definiteness is the major difference between a scientist and a drifter. Through the principle of definiteness of purpose and plan, the scientist forces nature to hand over her most profound secrets. It was through this principle that Edison uncovered the secret of the talking machine, the incandescent electric light, and scores of other benefits for mankind.

Q Then I understand that definiteness is the first requisite for success in all earthly undertakings? Is that right?

A Exactly! Anything which teaches people to examine facts and coordinate them into definite plans through accurate thinking is hard on my profession. If this thirst for definite knowledge now spreading over the world keeps up, my business will be shot to pieces within the next few centuries. I thrive on ignorance, superstition, intolerance, and fear, but I cannot stand up under definite knowledge properly organized into definite plans in the minds of people who think for themselves.

Q Why don't you take over Omnipotence and manage the whole works in your own way?

A You might as well ask why the negative portion of the electron doesn't take over the positive portion and run the entire works. The answer is that both the positive and the negative charges of energy are necessary to the existence of the electron. One is balanced equally against the other, stalemated, as it were.

So it is with what you call Omnipotence and I. We represent the positive and the negative forces of the entire system of universes, and we are equally balanced one against the other.

If this power of balance were shifted the slightest degree, the whole system of universes would become quickly reduced to a mass of inert matter. Now you know why I cannot take over the whole show and run it my way.

Q If what you say is true, you have exactly the same power as Omnipotence. Is that true?

A **That is correct. My opposition—you call it Omnipotence—expresses itself through the forces which you call good, the positive forces of nature. I express myself through the forces you call bad, the negative forces. Both good and bad are coincidental with existence. One is as important as the other.**

Q Then the doctrine of predestination is sound. People are born to success or failure, misery or happiness, to be good or bad, and they have nothing to do with this nor can they modify their natures. Is that your claim?

A **Emphatically not! Every human being has a wide range of choice in both his thoughts and his deeds. Every human being can use his brain for the reception and the expression of positive thoughts or he can use it for the expression of negative thoughts. His choice in this important matter shapes his entire life.**

Q From what you have said I gather the idea that human beings have more freedom of expression than either you or your opposition. Is that correct?

A **That is true. Omnipotence and I are bound by immutable laws of nature. We cannot express ourselves in any manner not conforming to these laws.**

Q Then it is true that man has rights and privileges not available to either Omnipotence or the Devil. Is that the truth?

A **Yes, that is true, but you might well have added that man has not yet fully awakened to the realization of this potential** power. Man still regards himself as something resembling the worms in the dust, when in reality he has more power than all other living things combined.

Q Definiteness of purpose seems to be a panacea for all evils of man.

A Not that perhaps, but you may be sure no one ever will become self-determining without it.

Q Why aren't children taught definiteness of purpose in the public schools?

A For the reason that there is no definite plan or purpose behind any of the school curricula! Children are sent to school to make credits and to learn how to memorize, not to learn what they want of life.

Says the Devil: ***"Children are sent to school to make credits and to learn how to memorize, not to learn what they want of life."***

\+ \+ \+ \+ \+ \+ \+ \+ \+ \+

Again, I find this chilling. Hill sounded this alarm in 1938 and yet the manuscript went unpublished and today we are still "teaching to the test" in our schools. I am on a mission to promote financial education to teach young people about money, a true life skill, and yet many schools still reject it because it does not satisfy the "test requirements" upon which they are graded and receive funding. Is it not time to sound the alarms again?

Q What good is a school credit if one cannot convert it into the material and spiritual needs of life?

A I am only a Devil, not an un-winder of riddles!

Q I deduce from all you say that neither the schools nor the churches prepare the youths of the world with a practical working knowledge of their own minds. Is anything of more importance to a human being than an understanding of the forces and circumstances which influence his own mind?

A The only thing of enduring value to any human being is a working knowledge of his own mind. The churches do not permit a person to inquire into the possibilities of his own mind, and the schools do not recognize that such a thing as a mind exists.

Why is Napoleon Hill so down on churches and the prevailing organized religions of his day? I believe his criticism stems from an abiding love for the true spirit and meaning of faith and the underlying validity of all religious traditions—despite what human beings do to weaken or corrupt them. What is the balance between accepting that which is revealed to your mind and heart—your soul—and the reality of life in a world so often infected with evil, as personified by Hill's Devil?

Q Aren't you a little hard on the schools and the churches?

A No, I am merely describing them as they are, without bias or prejudice.

Q Aren't the schools and the churches your bitter enemies?

A **Their leaders may think they are, but I am impressed only by facts. The truth is this, if you must know it: the churches are my most helpful allies and the schools run the churches a close second.**

Q On what specific or general grounds do you make this claim?

A **On the grounds that both the churches and the schools help me to convert people to the habit of drifting.**

Q Do you realize that your charge is substantially a sweeping indictment of the two institutions of major importance which have been responsible for civilization, in its present form?

A **Do I realize it? Man alive, I gloat over it. If the schools and churches had taught people how to think for themselves, where would I be, now?**

Q This confession of yours will disillusion millions of people whose only hope for salvation is in their churches. Isn't that a cruel thing to do to them? Wouldn't most people be better off living in the bliss of ignorance than to know the truth about you?

A **What do you mean by the term "salvation"? From what are people being saved? The only form of enduring salvation that is worth a green fig to any human being is that which comes from recognition of the power of his own mind. Ignorance and fear are the only enemies from which men need salvation.**

Q You seem to hold nothing sacred.

A **You are wrong. I hold sacred the one thing which is my master—the one thing I fear.**

Q What is that?

A **The power of independent thought backed by definiteness of purpose.**

Q Then you do not have many people to fear?

A **Only two out of every 100 to be exact. I control all others.**

Q Let's give the churches a rest and get back to the public schools. Your confession has shown clearly that you thrive and perpetuate yourself from one generation to another by the clever trick of taking over the minds of children before they have the chance to learn how to use their minds.

I wish to know what is wrong with a public school system that permits the Devil to control so many people. I wish to know, also, what can be done to the established system of teaching that will insure all children the opportunity to learn, first, that they have minds, and second, how to use those minds to bring spiritual and economic freedom.

I am putting the question to you definitely enough, and since you have stressed the importance of definiteness of purpose I am here and now putting you on notice that your answer to my question must be definite.

A **Wait a moment while I catch my breath. You have given me quite an order! It seems strange that you would come to the Devil to learn how to live. I should think you would go to my opposition. Why don't you?**

Q Your Majesty, it is you who are on trial here, not I. I want the truth and I am not particular as to the source from which I get it. There is something radically wrong with the system of education that has given us a balance sheet with life that shows us hopelessly in the red and groping for the road to self-determination as if we were so many animals lost in the jungle.

I want to know two things about this system. First, what is the major weakness of the system? Second, how can this weakness be eliminated? The floor is yours again! Please stick to the question and stop trying to decoy me into the discussion of deep, abstract subjects. That's definite, is it not?

A **You leave me no choice but that of direct answer. To begin with, the public school system approaches the subject of education from the wrong angle. The school system endeavors to teach children to memorize facts, instead of teaching them how to use their own minds.**

Q Is that all that is wrong with the system?

A **No, that is only the beginning. Another major weakness of the school system is that it does not establish in the minds of children either the importance of definiteness of purpose or make any attempt to teach youths how to be definite about anything.**

The major object of all schooling is to force the students to cram their memories with facts instead of teaching them how to organize and make practical use of facts.

This cramming system centers the attention of students on the accumulation of "credits" but overlooks the important question of how to use knowledge in the practical affairs of life. This system turns out graduates whose names are inscribed upon parchment certificates, but whose minds are empty of

self-determination. The school system got off to a bad start at the beginning. The schools began as institutions of "higher learning," operated entirely for the select few whose wealth and family entitled them to education.

Thus the entire school system was evolved by beginning at the top and working back down to the bottom. It is no wonder the system neglects to teach children the importance of definiteness of purpose when the system, itself, has literally evolved through indefiniteness.

Q What would correct this weakness of the public school system? Let's not complain of the weakness of the system unless we are prepared to offer a practical remedy with which it can be corrected. In other words, while we are discussing the importance of definiteness of plan and purpose, let us take our own medicine and be definite.

A **Why don't you lay off the schools and churches and save yourself plenty of trouble? Don't you know that you are poking your nose into the affairs of the two forces that control the world? Suppose you do show up the schools and the churches as being weak and inadequate for the needs of human beings? What then? With what are you going to replace these two institutions?**

Q Stop trying to evade my questions by the old trick of asking a counter-question! I do not propose to replace the schools and churches. But I do propose to find out, if I can, how these organized forces can be modified so they will serve people instead of keeping them in ignorance. Go ahead, now, and give me a detailed catalogue of all the changes in the public school system which would improve it.

A So you want the entire catalogue, do you? Do you want the suggested changes in the order of their importance?

This is another point at which the questioner forces the Devil out of his comfort zone. It is amusing and instructive to witness this exchange, which provides a roadmap for improvement of our public schools.

Q Describe the changes needed just as they come to you.

A You are forcing me to commit an act of treason against myself, but here it is:

> Reverse the present system by giving children the privilege of leading in their school work instead of following orthodox rules designed only to impart abstract knowledge. Let instructors serve as students and let the students serve as instructors.
>
> As far as possible, organize all school work into definite methods through which the student can learn by doing, and direct the class work so that every student engages in some form of practical labor connected with the daily problems of life.
>
> Ideas are the beginning of all human achievement. Teach all students how to recognize practical ideas that may be of benefit in helping them acquire whatever they demand of life.
>
> Teach the students how to budget and use time, and above

all teach the truth that time is the greatest asset available to human beings and the cheapest.

Teach the student the basic motives by which all people are influenced and show how to use these motives in acquiring the necessities and the luxuries of life.

Teach children what to eat, how much to eat, and what is the relationship between proper eating and sound health.

Teach children the true nature and function of the emotion of sex, and above all, teach them that it can be transmuted into a driving force capable of lifting one to great heights of achievement.

Teach children to be definite in all things, beginning with the choice of a definite major purpose in life!

Teach children the nature of and possibilities for good and evil in the principle of habit, using as illustrations with which to dramatize the subject the everyday experiences of children and adults.

Teach children how habits become fixed through the law of hypnotic rhythm, and influence them to adopt, while in the lower grades, habits that will lead to independent thought!

Teach children the difference between temporary defeat and failure, and show them how to search for the seed of an equivalent advantage which comes with every defeat.

Teach children to express their own thoughts fearlessly and to accept or reject, at will, all ideas of others, reserving to themselves, always, the privilege of relying upon their own judgment.

Teach children to reach decisions promptly and to change them, if at all, slowly and with reluctance, and never without a definite reason.

Teach children that the human brain is the instrument with which one receives, from the great storehouse of nature, the energy which is specialized into definite thoughts; that the brain does not think, but serves as an instrument for the interpretation of stimuli which cause thought.

Teach children the value of harmony in their own minds and that this is attainable only through self-control.

Teach children the nature and the value of self-control.

Teach children that there is a law of increasing returns which can be and should be put into operation, as a matter of habit, by rendering always more service and better service than is expected of them.

Teach children the true nature of the Golden Rule, and above all show them that through the operation of this principle, everything they do to and for another they do also to and for themselves.

Teach children not to have opinions unless they are formed from facts or beliefs which may reasonably be accepted as facts.

Teach children that cigarettes, liquor, narcotics, and over-indulgence in sex destroy the power of will and lead to the habit of drifting. Do not forbid these evils—just explain them.

Teach children the danger of believing anything merely because their parents, religious instructors, or someone else says it is so.

Teach children to face facts, whether they are pleasant or unpleasant, without resorting to subterfuge or offering alibis.

Teach children to encourage the use of their sixth sense through which ideas present themselves in their minds from unknown sources, and to examine all such ideas carefully.

Teach children the full import of the law of compensation as it was interpreted by Ralph Waldo Emerson, and show them how the law works in the small, everyday affairs of life.

Teach children that definiteness of purpose, backed by definite plans persistently and continuously applied, is the most efficacious form of prayer available to human beings.

Teach children that the space they occupy in the world is measured definitely by the quality and quantity of useful service they render the world.

Teach children there is no problem which does not have an appropriate solution and that the solution often may be found in the circumstance creating the problem.

Teach children that their only real limitations are those which they set up or permit others to establish in their own minds.

Teach them that man can achieve whatever man can conceive and believe!

Teach children that all schoolhouses and all textbooks are elementary implements which may be helpful in the development of their minds, but that the only school of real value is the great University of Life wherein one has the privilege of learning from experience.

Teach children to be true to themselves at all times and, since they cannot please everybody, therefore to do a good job of pleasing themselves.

Q That is an imposing list, but it seems conspicuous by the fact it ignores practically every subject now taught in the public schools. Was that intended?

A Yes. You asked for a list of suggested changes in public school curricula which would benefit children—well, that is what you got.

Q Some of the changes you suggest are so unorthodox they would shock most of the educators of today, wouldn't they?

A Most of the educators of today need to be shocked. A good sound shock often helps the brain that has been atrophied by habit.

Q Would the changes you suggest for the public schools give children immunity against the habit of drifting?

A Yes, that is one of the results the changes would bring, but there are others too.

I can't say that I agree with each thing on the Devil's list. However, when I stopped to analyze his list of recommendations, this question came to my mind: Isn't that what our schools should be teaching our children? The Devil knew this and we didn't?!?

I wish Hill had thought to ask why our schools are what they are—and where they are—or what and where they aren't. The great scholars who designed our system of schooling must have realized the importance of at least some of what the Devil professed our schools should be teaching. Why aren't these things part of the system? How could the original architects of what is today our compulsory education system have been so far off target? The Devil did make the claim that the school system is one of his primary vehicles for creating and sustaining his large army of drifters. Could it be?

Q How could the suggested changes be forced into the public school system? You know, of course, it is as difficult to get a new idea into an educator's brain as it is to interest a religious leader in modifying religion so it will help people to get more from life.

Any of you who have tried to work to make changes in the public school system are probably nodding right now.

A The quickest and surest way to force practical ideas into the public schools is to first introduce the ideas through private schools and establish such a demand for their use that public school officials will be compelled to employ them.

Q Should any other changes be made in the public school system?

A Yes, many. Among other changes needed in all public school programs is the addition of a complete course of training in the psychology of harmonious negotiation between people. All children should be taught how to sell their way through life with the minimum amount of friction.

Every public school should teach the principles of individual achievement through which one may attain a position of financial independence.

Classes should be abolished altogether. They should be replaced by the round table or conference system such as businessmen employ. All students should receive individual instruction and guidance in connection with subjects which cannot be properly taught in groups.

Every school should have an auxiliary group of instructors consisting of business and professional people, scientists, artists, engineers, and newspapermen, each of whom would impart to all the students a practical working knowledge of his own profession, business, or occupation. This instruction should be conducted through the conference system, to save the time of the instructors.

Q What you have suggested is, in effect, an auxiliary system of instruction that would give all school children a working knowledge of the practical affairs of life, direct from the original source. Is that the idea?

A You've stated it correctly.

This is another subject that strikes close to home. My husband recalls that during the early 1970s in New Jersey, one of the organizations that he was involved with assembled a

group of scientists and businessmen to teach basic courses—for example, mathematics and physics—in their fields as volunteers in the public schools, only to be told that since the scientists and businessmen were not professional teachers, they were not welcome. More recently, the mission of bringing practical teaching into the schools has been popularized by several groups (Teach for America, America Saves, Junior Achievement), but it is still often viewed as enhancement material and not part of the core curriculum.

This and many other shifts in how content, context, principles, and skills are delivered to our children in our compulsory system of education need to be included as part of an interactive, experiential process that will determine how our children live their lives—and what impact they will have on this complex world in which we live. The challenge is this: How do we package it all into a deliverable program that can be systematically and systemically implemented so it is success-oriented, rewarding, and fulfilling for all participants, children and adults alike? I am pleased and proud to say that I work with groups that have designed such programs—and they're taking these programs forward with definiteness of purpose.

Their vision of the future—like ours—is to have an educational system that evolves into a powerful force, capable of producing self-motivated, independent-thinking, self-reliant, contributing members of society. And capable also of producing something more important—future generations ready and able to work in a complex world, to live successfully, to take pleasure in empowering themselves and others, and to make a real and lasting difference in the world as informed, responsible, involved global citizens, each with definiteness of purpose!

Q Let us dismiss the public school system and go back to the churches for a moment. All my life I have heard clergymen preaching against sin and warning sinners to beware and repent so they could be saved. But I have never heard any of them tell me what sin is. Will you give me some light on this subject?

A Sin is anything one does or thinks which causes one to be unhappy! Human beings who are in sound physical and spiritual health should be at peace with themselves and always happy. Any form of mental or physical misery indicates the presence of sin.

Q Name some of the common forms of sin.

A It is a sin to overeat because that leads to ill health and misery.

It is a sin to over-indulge in sex because that breaks down one's will power and leads to the habit of drifting.

It is a sin to permit one's mind to be dominated by negative thoughts of envy, greed, fear, hatred, intolerance, vanity, self-pity, or discouragement, because these states of mind lead to the habit of drifting.

It is a sin to cheat, lie, and steal, because these habits destroy self-respect, subdue one's conscience, and lead to unhappiness.

It is a sin to remain in ignorance because that leads to poverty and loss of self-reliance.

It is a sin to accept from life anything one does not want because that indicates an unpardonable neglect to use the mind.

Q Is it a sin for one to drift through life, without definite aim, plan, or purpose?

A Yes, because this habit leads to poverty and destroys the privilege of self-determination. It also deprives one of the privilege of using his own mind as a medium of contact with Infinite Intelligence.

Q Are you the chief inspirer of sin?

A Yes! It is my business to gain control of the minds of people in every way possible.

Q Can you control the mind of a person who commits no sin?

A I cannot, because that person never permits his mind to be dominated by any form of negative thought. I cannot enter the mind of one who never sins, let alone control it.

Q What is the commonest and most destructive of all sins?

A Fear and ignorance.

Q Have you nothing else to add to the list?

A There is nothing else to be added.

Q What is faith?

A It is a state of mind wherein one recognizes and uses the power of positive thought as a medium by which one contacts and draws upon the universal store of Infinite Intelligence at will.

Q In other words, faith is the absence of all forms of negative thought. Is that the idea?

A Yes, that is another way of describing it.

Q Has a drifter the capacity to use faith?

A He may have the capacity but he does not use it. Everyone has the potential power to clear his mind of all negative thoughts and thereby avail himself of the power of faith.

Q Stating the matter in another way, faith is definiteness of purpose backed by belief in the attainment of the object of that purpose. Is that correct?

A That's the idea, exactly.

Faith is "a state of mind wherein one recognizes and uses the power of positive thought as a medium by which one contacts and draws upon the universal store of Infinite Intelligence at will."

\+ + + + + + + + + +

Hill succinctly sums up the definition:
"Faith is definiteness of purpose backed by belief in the attainment of the object of that purpose."

✦ *Chapter Ten* ✦

SELF-DISCIPLINE

Q WHAT PREPARATION MUST ONE UNDERGO before being able to move with definiteness of purpose at all times?

A One must gain *mastery over self.* This is the second of the seven principles. The person who is not master of himself can never be master of others. Lack of self-mastery is, of itself, the most destructive form of indefiniteness.

"The person who is not master of himself can never be master of others."

How true this is! Think of our political leaders who have fallen from grace because they could not control their own behavior. How can we trust them to control ours?

Q Where should one begin when making a start at control over self?

A By mastering the three appetites responsible for most of one's lack of self-discipline. The three appetites are (1) the desire for food, (2) the desire for expression of sex, (3) the desire to express loosely organized opinions.

Q Does man have other appetites which need control?

A Yes, many of them, but these three are the ones which should be conquered first. When a man becomes master of these three appetites, he has developed enough self-discipline to conquer easily those of lesser importance.

Q But these are natural appetites. They must be indulged if one is to be healthy and happy.

A To be sure they are natural appetites, but they are also dangerous because people who have not mastered themselves over-feed the appetites. Self-mastery contemplates sufficient control over the appetites to enable one to feed them what they need and withhold food not needed.

Q Your viewpoint is both interesting and educational. Describe the details through which I may understand how and under what circumstances people over-feed the appetites.

A Take the desire for physical food, for example. The majority of people are so weak in self-discipline they fill their stomachs with combinations of rich food which please the taste but over-work the organs of digestion and elimination.

They pour into their stomachs both quantity and combinations of food which the body chemist can dispose of only by converting the food into deadly toxic poisons.

These poisons clog and stagnate the body sewer system until it slows down in its work of elimination of waste matter. After a while the sewer system stops working altogether, and the victim has what he calls "constipation."

By that time he is ready for the hospital. Auto-intoxication, or body sewer poisoning, takes the machinery of the brain and rolls it into something resembling a wad of putty.

The victim then becomes sluggish in his physical movements and mentally irritable and fussy. If he could only take one good look at, and one bad smell of, his sewer system, he would be ashamed to look himself in the face.

City sewers are not the pleasantest of places when they become over-loaded or clogged, but they are clean and sweet compared with the intestinal sewer when it has been over-loaded or clogged. This is not a pretty story to be associated with the pleasant and necessary act of eating, but that is where it belongs because over-eating and wrong food combinations are the evils which cause auto-intoxication.

People who eat wisely and keep their body sewers clean handicap me because a clean body sewer generally means a sound body and a brain that functions properly.

Imagine—if your imagination can be stretched that far—how any human being could move with definiteness of purpose with his body sewer filled with enough poison to kill a hundred people if it were injected into their bloodstream directly.

Here again, Napoleon Hill is far ahead of his time. Science eventually caught up with Hill—and even surpassed his intuition about physical processes and how they link to mental and emotional health.

Q And all this trouble is the result of lack of control over the physical appetite for food?

A Well, if you wish to be absolutely correct you should say that improper eating is responsible for the majority of the ills of the body, and practically all headaches.

If you want proof of this, select 100 people suffering with headaches and give each of them a thorough washing out of their body sewer systems with a high enema, and observe

that no fewer than ninety-five of the headaches will disappear within a few minutes after their sewers have been cleaned.

Q From all you say about the intestinal tract, I gather the impression that mastery over the physical appetite for food means also mastery over the habit of neglecting to keep the intestines clean?

A **Yes, that is true. It is just as important to eliminate the waste matter of the body and the unused portions of food as it is to take the right amount and the correct combinations of food.**

Q I never thought of auto-intoxication as being one of your devices of control over people, and I am utterly shocked to know how many people are victims of this subtle enemy. Let's hear what you have to say of the other two appetites.

A **Well, take the desire for sex expression. Now there is a force with which I master the weak and the strong, the old and the young, the ignorant and the wise. In fact, I master all who neglect to master sex!**

Q How can one master the emotion of sex?

A **By the simple process of transmuting that emotion into some form of activity other than copulation. Sex is one of the greatest of all forces which motivate human beings. Because of this fact it is also one of the most dangerous forces. If humans would control their sex desires and transmute them into a driving force with which to carry on their occupation—that is, if they spent on their work one half the time they dissipate in pursuit of sex, they would never know poverty.**

Q Do I understand you to imply there is a relationship between sex and poverty?

A **Yes, where sex is not under definite control. If allowed to run its natural course, sex will quickly lead one into the habit of drifting.**

Q Is there any relationship between sex and leadership?

A **Yes, all great leaders in every walk of life are highly sexed, but they follow the habit of controlling their sex desires, switching them into a driving force behind their occupation.**

Q Is the habit of over-indulgence in sex as dangerous as the habit of taking narcotics or liquor?

A **There is no difference between these habits. Both lead to hypnotic control, through the habit of drifting!**

Q Why does the world look upon sex as something vulgar?

A **Because of the vulgar abuse people have made of this emotion. It is not sex that is vulgar. It is the individual who neglects or refuses to control and guide it.**

Q Do you mean, by your statement, that one should not indulge the desire for sex?

A **No, I mean that sex, like all other forces available to man, should be understood, mastered, and made to serve man. The desire for sex expression is as natural as the desire for food. The desire can no more be killed than one can entirely stop a river from flowing. If the emotion of sex is shut off from the natural mode of expression, it will break out in some other less desirable form, just as a river will, if dammed, break through** and flow around the dam. The person who has self-discipline understands the emotion of sex, respects it, and learns to control and transmute it into constructive activities.

Q Just what damage is there in over-indulgence of sex?

A The greatest damage is that it depletes the source of man's greatest driving force, and wastes, without adequate compensation, man's creative energy.

It dissipates energy needed by nature to maintain physical health. Sex is nature's most useful therapeutic force.

It depletes the magnetic energy which is the source of an attractive, pleasing personality.

It removes the sparkle from one's eyes and sets up discord in the tone of one's voice.

It destroys enthusiasm, subdues ambition, and leads inevitably to the habit of drifting on all subjects.

Q I would like for you to answer my question in another way by telling me what beneficial ends the emotion of sex may be made to attain, if mastered and transmuted.

A Controlled sex supplies the magnetic force that attracts people to one another. It is the most important factor of a pleasing personality.

It gives quality to the tone of voice and enables one to convey through the voice any feeling desired.

It serves, as nothing else can serve, to give motive-power to one's desires.

It keeps the nervous system charged with the energy needed to carry on the work of maintaining the body.

It sharpens the imagination and enables one to create useful ideas.

It gives quickness and definiteness to one's physical and mental movements.

It gives one persistence and perseverance in the pursuit of one's major purpose in life.

It is a great antidote for all fear.

It gives one immunity against discouragement.

It helps to master laziness and procrastination.

It gives one physical and mental endurance while undergoing any form of opposition or defeat.

It gives one the fighting qualities necessary under all circumstances for self-defense.

In brief, it makes winners and not quitters!

Q Are those all the advantages you claim for controlled sex energy?

A No, they are only some of the more important benefits it provides. Perhaps some will believe the greatest of all the virtues of sex is that it is nature's method of perpetuation of all living things. This alone should remove all thought that sex is vulgar.

Q I gather, from what you say, that the emotion of sex is a virtue, not a fault.

A It is a virtue when controlled and directed to the attainment of desirable ends. It is a fault when neglected and permitted to lead to acts of lust.

Q Why aren't these truths taught to children by their parents and the public schools?

A The neglect is due to ignorance of the real nature of sex.

It is just as necessary in maintaining health for one to understand and properly use the emotion of sex as it is to keep the body sewer system clean. Both subjects should be taught in all public schools and all homes where there are children.

Q Wouldn't the majority of parents need instruction on the proper function and use of sex before they could intelligently teach their children?

A Yes, and so would the public schoolteachers.

Q What relative position of importance would you give to the need for accurate knowledge on the subject of sex?

A It is next to the top of the list. There is but one thing of greater importance to human beings. That is accurate thought.

"There is but one thing of greater importance to human beings. That is accurate thought."

Q Do I understand you to say that knowledge of the true functions of sex and ability to think accurately are the two things of greatest importance to mankind?

A That is what I intended you to understand. Accurate thinking comes first because it is the solution to all man's problems, the answer to all his prayers, the source of opulence and all material possessions. Accurate thinking is aided by properly controlled and directed sex emotion because sex emotion is the same energy as that with which one thinks. It begins with those who desire self-determination sufficiently to be willing to pay its price. No one can be entirely free—spiritually, mentally, physically, and economically—without learning the art of accurate thinking. No one can learn to think accurately without including, as a part of the needed knowledge, information on the control of sex emotion through transmutation.

Q It will be a great surprise to many people to learn there is so close a relationship between thinking and sex emotion. Tell us, now, about the third appetite, and let's see what it has to do with self-discipline.

A The habit of expressing loosely organized opinions is one of the most destructive of habits. Its destructiveness consists in its tendency to influence people to guess instead of searching for the facts when they form opinions, create ideas, or organize plans.

The habit develops a grasshopper mind—one that jumps from one thing to another but never completes anything.

And of course, carelessness in the expression of opinions leads to the habit of drifting. From there it is only a step or two until one is bound by the law of hypnotic rhythm which automatically prohibits accurate thinking.

"The habit of expressing loosely organized opinions is one of the most destructive of habits."

Q What other disadvantages are there in free expression of opinions?

A The person who talks too much informs the world of his

aims and plans and gives to others the opportunity to profit by his ideas.

Wise men keep their plans to themselves and refrain from expressing uninvited opinions. This prevents others from appropriating their ideas and makes it difficult for others to interfere with their plans.

Q Why do so many people indulge in the habit of expressing uninvited opinions?

A The habit is one way of expressing egotism and vanity. The desire for self-expression is inborn in people. The motive behind the habit is to attract the attention of others and to impress them favorably. Actually it has just the opposite effect. When the self-invited speaker attracts attention, it usually is unfavorable.

Q Yes, what other disadvantages has the habit?

A The person who insists on talking seldom has an opportunity to learn by listening to others.

Q But isn't it true that a magnetic speaker often puts himself in the way of opportunity to benefit himself by attracting the attention of others through his powers of oratory?

A Yes, a magnetic orator does have an asset of tremendous value in his ability to impress people by his speech, but he cannot make the best use of this asset if he forces his speech on others without their invitation.

No single quality adds more to one's personality than the ability to speak with emotional feeling, force, and conviction, but the speaker must not impose his speech upon others without being invited to do so. There is an old saying that nothing is worth more than its actual cost. This applies as well to the free uninvited expression of opinions as to material things.

Q What about people who volunteer their opinions by expressing them in writing? Do they also suffer by lack of self-discipline?

A One of the worst pests on earth is the person who writes uninvited letters to people of prominence. Men in public office, moving picture stars, men who have succeeded in business or written a best-selling book, and people whose names appear often in the newspapers are continuously besieged by people who write letters expressing their opinion on all subjects.

Q But the writing of uninvited letters is a harmless way of finding pleasure through self-expression, is it not? What damage does one do by the habit?

Take a moment to remember that letter-writing was about the only way to communicate in the written form when Napoleon Hill wrote this manuscript. As you read, think about how his thoughts would apply to today's world of blogging and social networking.

A Habits are contagious. Every habit attracts a flock of its relatives. The habit of doing anything that is useless leads to the formation of other habits that are useless, especially the habit of drifting.

But that is not all the dangers associated with the habit of indulging in uninvited expression of opinions. The habit creates enemies and places in their hands dangerous weapons by which they may do great injury to the one who indulges in it. Thieves and confidence men and racketeers pay big prices for the names and addresses of the writers of uninvited letters, knowing as they do the writers of these letters become easy victims of all manner of schemes that result in the loss of their money. They refer to the writers of such letters as "nuts." If you wish to know how foolish people are who write uninvited letters, read the "nut column" of any newspaper—the column in which the paper publishes the voluntary opinions of its readers—and you will see for yourself how the writers of such letters antagonize people and invite opposition from others.

Q I had no idea, Your Majesty, that people get into so much difficulty through uninvited expression of their opinions, but now that you have brought up the subject I do remember writing the editor of a prominent magazine an uninvited letter of criticism which cost me a fine position on his staff, at a fat salary.

A That is a perfect example. The proper place to begin self-discipline is right where you stand. The way to begin is by recognizing the truth—that there is nothing for good or evil throughout the myriads of universes except the power of natural law. There is no individual personality anywhere throughout the myriad of universes with the slightest power to influence a human being save nature and human beings themselves.

There is no human being now living, no human being has ever lived, and no human being ever will live with the right or the power to deprive another human being of the inborn privilege of free and independent thought. That privilege is the only one over which any human being can have absolute control. No adult human being ever loses the right to freedom of thought, but most humans lose the benefits of this privilege either by neglect or because it has been taken away from them by their parents or religious instructors before the age of understanding. These are self-evident truths, no less important because they are being called to your attention by the Devil than they would be if brought to your attention by my opposition.

Hill distinguishes our right to have independent thoughts from our uninvited expression of those thoughts. How would you apply this principle in today's world of blogging and social media?

Q But what are people going to lean upon in the hour of emergency when they know not where nor to whom to appeal?

A Let them lean upon the only dependable power available to any human being.

Q And what is that?

A Themselves! The power of their own thoughts. The only power they can control and may rely upon. The only power which cannot be perverted, colored, modified, and falsified by their dishonest fellow human beings.

"The only dependable power available to any human being... The power of their own thoughts. The only power they can control and may rely upon."

+ + + + + + + + + +

You may not be able to control other people... but you can control how you react to them and their actions. This is an easy thing to say but much more difficult to do. We tend to want to change other people when we can truly only change ourselves and how we react to others.

Q All you say seems logical, but why must I come to the Devil to discover such profound truths? Let's get back to the seven principles. You have already disclosed enough information to show clearly that the secret of how to break the power of hypnotic rhythm is wrapped in the seven principles. You have shown, too, that the most important of these principles is self-discipline. Now go ahead and describe the other five principles you have not yet mentioned, and indicate what part they play in giving one self-discipline.

A First, let me summarize that part of my confession we have already covered.

I have frankly told you that my two most effective devices for mastering human beings are the habit of drifting and the law of hypnotic rhythm. I have shown you that drifting is not a natural law, but a man-made habit which leads to man's submission to the law of hypnotic rhythm.

The seven principles are the media by which man may break the hold of hypnotic rhythm and take possession, again, of his own mind. You see, therefore, the seven principles are the seven steps which lead victims of hypnotic rhythm out of the self-made prisons in which they are bound.

Q The seven principles are the master key that unlocks the door to spiritual, mental, and economic self-determination? Is that true?

A Yes, that's another way of stating the truth.

Chapter Eleven

LEARNING FROM ADVERSITY

Q Is failure ever a benefit to man?

A Yes. Indeed, learning from adversity is the third of the seven principles. But few people know that every adversity brings with it the seed of an equivalent advantage. Still fewer people know the difference between temporary defeat and failure. If this knowledge were generally known, I would be deprived of one of my strongest weapons of control over human beings.

Q But I understood you to say that failure is one of your greatest allies. I got the impression from your confession that failure causes people to lose ambition and quit trying, and then you take them over without opposition on their part.

A That is just the point. I take them over after they quit trying. If they knew the difference between temporary defeat and failure, they would not quit when they meet with opposition from life. If they knew that every form of defeat, and all failures, bring with them the seed of unborn opportunity, they would keep on fighting and win. Success usually is but one short step beyond the point where one quits fighting.

Q Is that all one might learn from adversity, defeat, and failure?

A No, that is the least of what one might learn. I hate to tell you this, but failure often serves as a blessing in disguise because it breaks the grip of hypnotic rhythm and frees the mind for a fresh start.

Q Now we are getting somewhere. So you have confessed, at long last, that even nature's law of hypnotic rhythm can be and often is annulled by nature herself. Is that correct?

A No, that is not stating the matter accurately. Nature never reverses any of her natural laws. Nature does not take away a human being's freedom of thought through hypnotic rhythm. The individual gives up his freedom by abuse of this law. If a man jumped from a tree and was killed by the sudden impact of his body with the earth, through the law of gravity, you wouldn't say nature murdered him, would you? You would say the man neglected to relate himself properly to the law of gravity.

Q I am beginning to see. The law of hypnotic rhythm is capable of both negative and positive application. It may drag one down to slavery through loss of the privilege of freedom of thought, or it may help one rise to great heights of achievement through the free use of thought, depending on how the individual relates himself to the law. Is that correct?

A Now you have it right.

Q But what about failure? One does not fail intentionally, with purpose aforethought. No one encourages temporary defeat. These are circumstances over which the individual often has no control whatsoever. How, then, can it be said that nature does not take away one's freedom of thought when failure destroys ambition, will power, and the self-confidence essential to make a fresh start?

A Failure is a man-made circumstance. It is never real until it has been accepted by man as permanent. Stating it another way, failure is a state of mind; therefore, it is something an individual can control until he neglects to exercise this privilege. Nature does not force people to fail. But nature does impose her law of hypnotic rhythm upon all minds and through this law gives permanency to the thoughts which dominate those minds.

In other words, failure thoughts are taken over by the law of hypnotic rhythm and made permanent if the individual accepts any circumstances as being permanent failure. That same law just as readily takes over and makes permanent thoughts of success.

"Failure is a state of mind; therefore, it is something an individual can control until he neglects to exercise this privilege."

+ + + + + + + + + +

Can this be true? Has Hill convinced you that "failure is a man-made circumstance"? I believe he makes a compelling case. If I look closely at my life—my own successes and failures in business, mistakes, and missteps—can I claim that anyone is responsible other than myself? Will a personal inventory of your life yield different results? Hill has helped me place a different value on failure than I did in the past...

Q What part, then, does failure play in helping an individual break the grip of hypnotic rhythm after that law has been fastened upon his mind?

A Failure brings a climax in which one has the privilege of clearing his mind of fear and making a new start in another direction. Failure proves conclusively that something is wrong with one's aims or the plans by which the object of these aims is sought. Failure is the dead end of the habit-path one has been following, and when it is reached it forces one to leave that path and take up another, thereby creating a new rhythm.

But failure does more than this. It gives an individual an opportunity to test himself wherein he may learn how much will power he possesses. Failure also forces people to learn many truths they would never discover without it. Failure often leads an individual to an understanding of the power of self-discipline without which no one could turn back after having once been the victim of hypnotic rhythm.

Study the lives of all people who achieve outstanding success in any calling and observe, with profit, that their success is usually in exact ratio to their experiences of defeat before succeeding.

"Failure brings a climax in which one has the privilege of clearing his mind of fear and making a new start in another direction."

Q Is this all you have to say of the advantages of failure?

A No, I have barely begun. If you want the real significance of adversity, failure, defeat, and all other experiences which break up a human being's habits and force him to form new habits, watch nature at her work. Nature uses illness to break the physical rhythm of the body when the cells and organs become improperly related. She uses economic depressions to break the rhythm of mass thought when great numbers of people become improperly related—through business, social, and political activities. And she uses failure to break the rhythm of negative thought when an individual becomes improperly related to himself in his own mind.

Observe carefully and you will see that everywhere in nature there is always at work a natural law which gives eternal change to all matter, all energy, and to the power of thought. The only permanent thing in the universes is change. Eternal, inexorable change—through which every atom of matter and every unit of energy has the opportunity to properly relate itself to all other units of matter and energy, and every human being has the opportunity and the privilege of properly relating himself to all other human beings no matter how many mistakes he makes, or how many times or in what ways he may be defeated.

When mass failure overtakes a nation, such as the 1929 world business depression, the circumstance is in perfect harmony with nature's plan to break up man's habits and give out fresh opportunities.

The beauty of publishing this book now, during the current economic turmoil, is that nature is once again breaking up man's habits and presenting fresh opportunities.

Q What you are saying intrigues me. Am I to understand that hypnotic rhythm has something to do with the way people relate themselves to one another?

A That abstract, elusive thing called character is nothing but a manifestation of the law of hypnotic rhythm; therefore, when speaking of one's character it would be proper to say his thought-habits have been crystallized into a positive or a negative personality, through hypnotic rhythm. One is good or bad because of the knitting together of his thoughts and deeds through hypnotic rhythm. One is bound by poverty or blessed with abundance because his aims, plans, and desires, or lack of them, have been made permanent and real by hypnotic rhythm.

Q Is that all you have to say of the connection between hypnotic rhythm and human relationships?

A No, I have just begun. Remember while I am talking I am speaking of the influence of hypnotic rhythm in connection with all human relationships. Men who succeed in business do so entirely because of the way they relate themselves to their associates and to others outside of the business.

Professional men who succeed do so largely because of the manner in which they relate themselves to their clients. It is much more important for the lawyer to know people and to know the laws of nature than it is to know the law. And the doctor is a failure before he starts unless he knows how to relate himself to his patients so as to establish their faith in him.

Marriage succeeds or fails entirely because of the manner in which the participants relate themselves to one another. Proper relationship in marriage begins with a proper motive for the marriage. Most marriages do not bring happiness because the contracting parties neither understand, nor attempt to understand, the law of hypnotic rhythm, through the operation of which every word they speak, every act in which they engage, and every motive by which they are inspired to deal with each other is picked up and woven into a web that entangles them in controversial misery or gives to them the wings of freedom through which they soar above all forms of unhappiness.

Every newly made acquaintanceship between people ripens into friendship and then into spiritual harmony (sometimes called love) or plants a germ of suspicion and doubt which evolves and grows into open rebellion, according to the way in which the participants in the acquaintanceship relate themselves to one another.

Hypnotic rhythm picks up the dominating motives, aims, purposes, and feelings of the contacting minds and weaves these into some degree of faith or fear, love or hatred. After the pattern has taken definite shape, as it does with time, it is forced upon the contacting minds and made a part thereof.

In this silent way does nature make permanent the dominating factors of every human relationship. In every human relationship the evil motives and the evil deeds of the contacting individuals are coordinated and consolidated into definite form and subtly woven into that all-important human trait known as character. In the same manner, the motives and the deeds of good are consolidated and forced upon the individual. You see, therefore, it is not only one's deeds but also one's very thoughts which determine the nature of all human relationships.

Q You are leading into pretty deep water. Let's keep near the shore, where I can follow you without fear of getting beyond a safe depth. Go ahead and tell me how this subject of human relationships actually works in the current affairs of a problem-filled world such as we have today.

A That is a happy thought. But let me make sure you understand the principles I am telling about, before I try to show you how to apply them in the affairs of life.

I wish to be sure you understand that the law of hypnotic rhythm is something that no one can control, influence, or evade. But everyone can relate himself to this law so as to benefit by its inexorable operation. Harmonious relationship with the law consists entirely of the individual changing his habits so they represent the circumstances and the things the individual wants and is willing to accept.

No one can change the law of hypnotic rhythm any more than one can change the law of gravity, but everyone can change himself. Remember, therefore, in all the discussion of this subject that all human relationships are made and maintained by the habits of the individuals related.

"No one can change the law of hypnotic rhythm any more than one can change the law of gravity, but everyone can change himself."

+ + + + + + + + + +

Have you ever tried to change someone else and only been frustrated when you realized you were not in control and therefore not succeeding?

The law of hypnotic rhythm plays only the part of solidifying the factors which constitute human relationships, but it does not create those factors. Before we go further with the discussion of human relationships, I want you to get a clear understanding of the subconscious mind.

The term "subconscious mind" represents a hypothetical physical organ which has no actual existence. The mind of man consists of universal energy (some call it Infinite Intelligence) which the individual receives, appropriates, and organizes in definite thought forms through the network of intricate physical apparatus known as a brain.

These thought forms are replicas of various stimuli which reach the brain through the five commonly known physical senses and the sixth sense, which is not so well known. When any form of stimuli reaches the brain and takes the definite shape of thought, it is classified and stored away in a group of the brain cells known as the memory group.

All thoughts of a similar nature are stored together so that the bringing forth of one leads to easy contact with all its associates. The system is very similar to the modern office filing cabinet, and it is operated in a similar manner.

The thought impressions with which one mixes the greatest amount of emotion (or feeling) are the dominating factors of the brain because they are always near the surface—at the top of the filing system, so to speak—where they spring into action voluntarily, the moment an individual neglects to exercise self-discipline. These emotion-laden thoughts are so powerful they often cause an individual to rush into action and indulge in deeds which have not been submitted to or approved by his reasoning faculty. These emotional outbursts usually destroy harmony in all human relationships. The brain often brings together combinations of emotional feeling so powerful they completely set aside the control of the reasoning faculty. On all such occasions human relationships are apt to be lacking in harmony.

Through the operation of the sixth sense, the brain of a human being may contact the filing cabinet of other brains and inspect at will whatever thought impressions are on file there. The condition under which one person may contact and inspect the filing cabinet of another person's brain is generally known as harmony, but you may better understand what is meant if I say brains attuned to the same rate of thought vibrations can easily and quickly exercise the privilege of entering and inspecting each other's filing cabinets of thoughts.

In addition to receiving organized thoughts from the filing cabinets of other brains through the sixth sense, one can, through this same physical organ, contact and receive information from the universal storehouse known as Infinite Intelligence.

All information reaching one's brain through the sixth sense comes from sources not easily isolated or traced; therefore, this sort of information is generally believed to come from one's subconscious mind. The sixth sense is the organ of the brain through which one receives all information, all knowledge, all thought impressions which do not come through one or more of the five physical senses.

Now that you understand how the mind operates, you will more easily understand how and why people come to grief through improper human relationships. You will also understand how human relationship may be made to yield riches in their highest form, riches in material, mental, and spiritual estates.

Moreover, you will understand there can never be happiness except through understanding and application of the right principles of human relationships. You will understand, too, that no individual is an entity unto himself, that completeness of mind can be attained only by harmony of purpose and deed between two or more minds. You will understand why every human being should, of his own choice, become his brother's keeper in fact as well as in theory.

Q What you say may be true, but I still insist that you have me beyond safe depths of thought. Let us get back nearer to the shore, where I can wade in familiar water. We shall go out into the deeper water after we learn to swim well. We started out to discuss the subject of how to profit by adversity, but it seems we have drifted somewhat afield from that subject.

A We have detoured, but we have not drifted. The Devil never drifts. The detour was necessary in order that you might be prepared to understand the most important part of this entire interview.

We are now ready to get back to the discussion of the subject of adversity. Inasmuch as most adversities grow out of improper relationships between people, it seems important to understand how people may become properly related.

Naturally the question arises as to what is a proper relationship between people? The answer is that the proper relationship is one that brings to all connected with it, or affected by it, some form of benefit.

"The proper relationship is one that brings to all connected with it, or affected by it, some form of benefit."

✦ ✦ ✦ ✦ ✦ ✦ ✦ ✦ ✦ ✦

Take a moment to inventory your relationships, at home, at work, and at play. List the relationships that seem in need of improvement and keep them in your mind as you continue reading.

Q What, then, is an improper relationship?

A Any relationship between people which damages anyone or brings any form of misery or unhappiness to any of the individuals.

Q How can improper relationships be corrected?

A By change of mind of the person causing the improper relationship, or by changing the persons to the relationship. Some minds harmonize naturally while others just as naturally clash. Successful human relationships, to endure as such, must be formed of minds that naturally harmonize, quite aside from the question of having common interests as a means of bringing them into harmony.

When you speak of business leaders who succeed because "they know how to pick men," you might more correctly say they succeed because they know how to associate minds which harmonize naturally. Knowing how to pick people successfully for any definite purpose in life is based upon ability to recognize the types of people whose minds naturally harmonize.

Remember Hill's definition of the Master Mind: *"harmonious coordination of two or more minds working to a definite end."*

Q Stay focused on adversity, if you will. If there are possible benefits to be found through adversity, name some of them.

A Adversity relieves people of vanity and egotism. It discourages selfishness by proving that no one can succeed without the cooperation of others.

Adversity forces an individual to test his mental, physical, and spiritual strength; it thus brings him face to face with his weaknesses and gives him the opportunity to bridge them.

Adversity forces one to seek ways and means to definite ends by meditation and introspective thought. This often leads to the discovery and use of the sixth sense through which one may communicate with Infinite Intelligence.

Adversity forces one to recognize the need for intelligence not available except from sources outside of one's own mind.

Adversity breaks old habits of thought and gives one an opportunity to form new habits; therefore, it may serve to break the hold of hypnotic rhythm and change its operation from negative to positive ends.

Q What is the greatest benefit one may receive through adversity?

A The greatest benefit of adversity is that it may, and generally does, force one to change one's thought-habits, thus breaking and redirecting the force of hypnotic rhythm.

Q In other words, failure always is a blessing when it forces one to acquire knowledge or to build habits that lead to the achievement of one's major purpose in life. Is that correct?

A Yes, and something more! Failure is a blessing when it forces one to depend less upon material forces and more upon spiritual forces.

Many human beings discover their "other selves," the forces which operate through the power of thought, only after some catastrophe deprives them of the full and free use of their physical bodies. When a man can no longer use his hands and his feet, he usually begins to use his brain; thus he puts himself in the way of discovering the power of his own mind.

The Devil brings in the "other self" here, revealing how we can use our power of thought and our "other selves" to discover our true power and major purpose.

Q What benefits may be derived from the loss of material things—money, for example?

A The loss of material things may teach many needed lessons, none greater, however, than the truth that man has control over nothing and has no assurance of the permanent use of anything except his own power of thought.

Q I wonder if this is not the greatest benefit available through adversity?

A No, the greatest potential benefit of any circumstance which causes one to make a fresh start is that it provides an opportunity to break the grip of hypnotic rhythm and set up a new set of thought-habits. New habits offer the only way out for people who fail. Most people who escape from the negative to the positive operation of the law of hypnotic rhythm do so only because of some form of adversity which forces them to change their thought-habits.

Q Isn't adversity apt to break one's self-reliance and cause one to give up hope?

A It has that effect on those whose will power is weak through long established habits of drifting. It has the opposite effect on those who have not been weakened through drifting. The non-drifter meets with temporary defeat and failure, but his reaction to all forms of adversity is positive. He fights instead of giving up, and usually wins.

Life gives no one immunity against adversity, but life gives to everyone the power of positive thought, which is sufficient to master all circumstances of adversity and convert them into benefits. The individual is left with the privilege of using or neglecting to use his prerogative right to think his way through all adversities. Every individual is forced either to use his thought power for the attainment of definite, positive ends, or by neglect or design use this power for the attainment of negative ends. There can be no compromise, no refusal to use the mind.

The law of hypnotic rhythm forces every individual to give some degree of use, either negative or positive, to his mind, but it does not influence the individual as to which use he will make of his mind.

"The non-drifter meets with temporary defeat and failure, but his reaction to all forms of adversity is positive. He fights instead of giving up, and usually wins."

+ + + + + + + + + +

Do you remember a time when you felt like giving up . . . but didn't? My co-author and I expand this concept in our book *Three Feet from Gold*, with stories of perseverance and never giving up from over thirty-five of today's top leaders, non-drifters of our time!

Q Am I to understand from what you say that every adversity is a blessing?

A No, I did not say that. I said there is the seed of an equivalent advantage in every adversity. I did not say there was the full-blown flower of advantage, just the seed. Usually the seed consists of some form of knowledge, some idea or plan, or some opportunity which would not have been available except through the change of thought-habits forced by the adversity.

Q Are those all the benefits available to human beings through failure?

A No, failure is used by nature as a common language in which she chastises people when they neglect to adapt themselves to her laws.

For example, the world war was man-made and destructive. Nature planted in the circumstances of the war the seed of an equivalent reprimand in the form of a world depression. The depression was inevitable and inescapable. It followed the war as naturally as day follows night and by the operation of the self-same law, the law of hypnotic rhythm.

Q Am I to understand that the law of hypnotic rhythm is the same as that which Ralph Waldo Emerson called the law of compensation?

A The law of hypnotic rhythm is the law of compensation. It is the power with which nature balances negative and positive forces throughout the universes, in all forms of energy, in all forms of matter, and in all human relationships.

Q Does the law of hypnotic rhythm operate quickly in all instances? For example, does this law immediately bless one with the benefits of positive application of thoughts, or curse one immediately with the results of negative thoughts?

A The law operates definitely but not always swiftly. Both the benefits and the penalties incurred through the law by individuals may be harvested by others, either before or after their death.

Observe how this law works by forcing upon one generation of people the effects of both the sins and the virtues of preceding generations. In the operation of all of nature's laws, the fourth dimension, time, is an inexorable factor. The length of time consumed by nature in the relation of effects to their causes depends, in every instance, on the circumstances at hand. Nature grows a pumpkin in three months. A good size oak tree requires a hundred years. She converts a hen's egg into a chicken in four weeks, but she requires nine months to convert the egg of a human being into an individual.

"Life gives no one immunity against adversity, but life gives to everyone the power of positive thought, which is sufficient to master all circumstances of adversity and convert them into benefits."

✦ ✦ ✦ ✦ ✦ ✦ ✦ ✦ ✦ ✦

Has nature created the current economic turmoil to allow us once again to convert our own personal adversities into benefits?

Chapter Twelve

ENVIRONMENT, TIME, HARMONY, AND CAUTION

Q I NOW HAVE A BETTER UNDERSTANDING of the potentialities of adversity and failure. You may go ahead, now, with your description of the next of the seven principles. What is your next principle?

A **The next principle is *environmental influence.***

Q Go ahead and describe the working principle of environmental influences as a determining factor in human destinies.

A **Environment consists of all the mental, spiritual, and physical forces which affect and influence human beings.**

Q What connection, if any, is there between environmental influences and hypnotic rhythm?

A **Hypnotic rhythm solidifies and makes permanent the thought-habits of human beings. Thought-habits are stimulated by environmental influences. In other words, the material on which thoughts are fed comes from one's environment. Thought-habits are made permanent by hypnotic rhythm.**

Q What is the most important part of one's environment, the part which determines, more than all others, whether an individual makes positive or negative use of his mind?

A **The most important part of one's environment is that created by his association with others. All people absorb and take over, either consciously or unconsciously, the thought-habits of those with whom they associate closely.**

Q Do you mean by this that constant association with a person whose thought-habits are negative influences one to form negative thought-habits?

A Yes, the law of hypnotic rhythm forces every human being to form thought-habits which harmonize with the dominating influences of his environment, particularly that part of his environment created by his association with other minds.

Q Then it is important that one select one's close associates with great care?

A Yes, one's intimate associates should be chosen with as much care as one chooses the food with which he feeds his body, with the object always of associating with people whose dominating thoughts are positive, friendly, and harmonious.

Q Which class of associates has the greatest influence upon one?

A One's partner in marriage and in the home and one's associates in his occupation. After that come close friends and acquaintances. Casual acquaintances and strangers have but little influence on one.

"The material on which thoughts are fed come from one's environment. Thought-habits are made permanent by hypnotic rhythm."

+ + + + + + + + + +

Have you ever felt your attitude or mood become negative just by being in the presence of someone negative? Was it your spouse, child, or business partner? Hill suggests that you need to interject thoughts that are positive, friendly, and harmonious not only to counteract those negative thoughts

but also to influence that person into a more positive space. If it is your business partner, evaluate if the relationship is one you want to save... or make the decision to move away from the partner's negativity.

Q Why does one's partner in marriage have so great an influence upon one's mind?

A Because the relationship of marriage brings people under the influence of spiritual forces of such weight that they become dominating forces of the mind.

Q How may environmental influences be used to break the grip of hypnotic rhythm?

A All influences which establish thought-habits are given permanency through the law of hypnotic rhythm. One may change the influences of his environment so that the dominating influences are either positive or negative, and the law of hypnotic rhythm will make them permanent, unless they are changed through one's habits of thought.

Q Stating this truth in another way, one may submit himself to any environmental influence desired, whether positive or negative, and the law of hypnotic rhythm will make the influence permanent when it assumes the magnitude of thought-habit. Is that the way the law works?

A That is correct. Be careful of all forces which inspire thought; those are the forces which constitute environment and determine the nature of one's earthly destiny.

Q What class of people controls their environmental influences?

A The non-drifters. All who are victims of the habit of drifting forfeit their power to choose their own environment. They become the victims of every negative influence of their environment.

Q Is there no way out for the drifter? Is there no method by which he may submit himself to the influence of a positive environment?

A Yes, there is a way out for drifters. They can stop drifting, take possession of their own minds, and choose an environment which inspires positive thought. This they may accomplish through definiteness of purpose.

Q Is that all there is to the act of eliminating the habit of drifting? Is the habit only a state of mind?

A Drifting is nothing but a negative state of mind, a state of mind conspicuous by its emptiness of purpose.

Q What effective procedure may one follow in establishing an environment most helpful in developing and maintaining positive thought-habits?

A The most effective of all environments is that which may be created by a friendly alliance of a group of people who will obligate themselves to assist one another in achieving the object of some definite purpose. This sort of an alliance is known as a Master Mind. Through its operation one may associate himself with carefully chosen individuals each of whom brings to the alliance some knowledge, experience, education, plan, or idea suited to his needs in carrying out the object of his definite purpose.

The most successful leaders in all walks of life avail themselves of this sort of made-to-order environmental influence. Outstanding achievement is impossible without the friendly cooperation of others. Stating the truth in another way, successful people must control their environment, thereby insuring themselves against the influence of a negative environment.

Q What of people whose duty to relatives makes it impossible for them to avoid the influence of a negative environment?

A No human being owes another any degree of duty which robs him of his privilege of building his thought-habits in a positive environment. On the other hand, every human being is duty bound to himself to remove from his environment every influence which even remotely tends to develop negative thought-habits.

Q Isn't this a cold-blooded philosophy?

A Only the strong survive. No one can be strong without removing himself from all influences which develop negative thought-habits. Negative thought-habits result in the loss of the privilege of self-determination, no matter what or who may cause those habits. Positive thought-habits may be controlled by the individual and made to serve his aims and purposes. Negative thought-habits control the individual and deprive him of the privilege of self-determination.

Q I deduce from all you have said that those who control the environmental influences out of which their thought-habits are built are masters of their earthly destinies and that all others are mastered by earthly destinies. Is that stating the matter correctly?

A **Perfectly stated.**

Q What establishes one's thought-habits?

A **All habits are established because of inherent or acquired desires, or motives. That is, habits are begun as the result of some form of definite desire.**

Q What takes place in the physical brain while one is forming thought-habits?

A **Desires are organized impulses of energy called thoughts. Desires that are mixed with emotional feeling magnetize the brain cells in which they are stored and prepare those cells to be taken over and directed by the law of hypnotic rhythm. When any thought appears in the brain or is created there, and is mixed with keen emotional feeling of desire, the law of hypnotic rhythm begins, at once, to translate it into its physical counterpart. Dominating thoughts, which are acted upon first by the law of hypnotic rhythm, are those with which are mixed the strongest desires and the most intense feelings. Thought-habits are established by the repetition of the same thoughts.**

Q What are the most impelling basic motives or desires which inspire thought action?

A **The ten most common motives, those which inspire most of one's thought-action, are these:**

- **The desire for sex expression and love**

- The desire for physical food
- The desire for spiritual, mental, and physical self-expression
- The desire for perpetuation of life after death
- The desire for power over others
- The desire for material wealth
- The desire for knowledge
- The desire to imitate others
- The desire to excel others
- The seven basic fears

These are the dominating motives which inspire the majority of all human endeavors.

Q What about the negative desires such as greed, envy, avarice, jealousy, anger? Are these not expressed more often than any of the positive desires?

A All negative desires are nothing but frustrations of positive desires. They are inspired by some form of defeat, failure, or neglect by human beings to adapt themselves to nature's laws in a positive way.

Q That's a new slant on the subject of negative thoughts. If I correctly understand what you have said, all negative thoughts are inspired by one's neglect or failure to adapt oneself harmoniously to nature's laws. Is that correct?

A That is exactly correct. Nature will not tolerate idleness or vacuums of any sort. All space must be and is filled with something.

Everything in existence, of both a physical and a spiritual nature, must be and is constantly in motion. The human brain is no exception. It was created to receive, organize, specialize, and express the power of thought. When the individual does not use the brain for the expression of positive, creative thoughts, nature fills the vacuum by forcing the brain to act upon negative thoughts.

There can be no idleness in the brain. Understand this principle and you will come into a new and important understanding of the part environmental influences take in the lives of human beings.

You will better understand, also, how the law of hypnotic rhythm operates, it being the law which keeps everything and everyone constantly moving through some form of expression of either negative or positive principles.

"Nature will not tolerate idleness or vacuums of any sort. All space must be and is filled with something... When the individual does not use the brain for the expression of positive, creative thoughts, nature fills the vacuum by forcing the brain to act upon negative thoughts."

+ + + + + + + + + +

I find this so true particularly when I think of children who have too much idle time on their hands. Don Green, CEO of the Napoleon Hill Foundation, remembers, "As young people we were constantly kept busy with the admonition that idleness was the devil's workshop." Interesting parallel, don't you think?

Nature is not interested in morals as such. She is not interested in right and wrong. She is not interested in justice and injustice. She is interested only in forcing everything to express action according to its nature!

Q That is an enlightening interpretation of nature's ways. To whom may I turn for corroboration of your claims?

A To men of science, to the philosophers, to all accurate thinkers. Lastly, to the physical manifestations of nature herself.

Nature has no such thing as dead matter. Every atom of matter is constantly in a state of motion. All energy is constantly in motion. There are no dead voids anywhere. Time and space are literally manifestations of motion of such swiftness that it cannot be measured by human beings.

Q Alas, one is forced to the conclusion, from what you say, that the sources of dependable knowledge are shockingly limited.

A The developed sources of knowledge are limited. Every normal adult human brain is a potential gateway to all the knowledge there is throughout the universes. Every normal adult brain has within its mechanism the possibility of direct communication with Infinite Intelligence, wherein exists all the knowledge that is or can ever be.

Q Your statement leads me to believe that human beings may become all they have attributed to what they call God. Is that what you mean?

A Through the law of evolution the human brain is being

perfected to communicate at will with Infinite Intelligence. The perfection will come through organized development of the brain, through its adaptation to nature's laws. Time is the factor which will bring perfection.

Q What causes cycles of recurring events, such as epidemics of disease, business depressions, wars, and crime waves?

A All such epidemics in which great numbers of people are similarly affected are caused by the law of hypnotic rhythm, through which nature consolidates thoughts of a similar nature and causes those thoughts to be expressed through mass action.

Q Then the Great Depression was put into motion because great numbers of people were influenced to release thoughts of fear. Is that correct?

A Perfectly. Millions of people were endeavoring to get something for nothing, through stock gambling. When they suddenly discovered they had gotten nothing for something, they became frightened, rushed to their banks to draw out their balances, and the panic was on. Through mass thought of millions of minds, all thinking in terms of fear of poverty, the depression was prolonged over a period of years.

The current economic turmoil in the United States and throughout the world was put into motion in a similar fashion. Millions were endeavoring to get something for nothing, through real estate (no-money-down deals, subprime mortgages, and valuation bubbles) as well as the

financial markets. When everything started to collapse, they became frightened and the panic was on once again. By changing the thoughts of these millions from fear back to focus on fundamentally sound financial principles, can we stabilize the economy? Napoleon Hill's philosophy can show us the way. The choice is ours.

Q From what you say, I deduce that nature consolidates the dominating thoughts of people and expresses these thoughts through some form of mass action, such as business depressions, business booms, and so on. Is that correct?

A You have the right idea.

Q Let us now take up the next of the seven principles. Go ahead and describe it.

A The next principle is *time*, the fourth dimension.

Q What relationship is there between time and the operation of the law of hypnotic rhythm?

A Time is the law of hypnotic rhythm. The lapse of time required to give permanency to thought-habits depends upon the object and the nature of the thoughts.

Q But I understood you to say that the only enduring thing in nature is change. If that is true, then time is constantly changing, rearranging, and recombining all things, including one's thought-habits. How, then, could the law of hypnotic rhythm give permanency to one's thought-habits?

A Time divides all thought-habits into two classes, negative thoughts and positive thoughts. One's individual thoughts are of course constantly changing and being recombined to suit the individual's desires, but thoughts do not change from negative to positive or vice versa except through voluntary effort on the part of the individual.

Time penalizes the individual for all negative thoughts and rewards him for all positive thoughts, according to the nature and purpose of the thoughts. If one's dominating thoughts are negative, time penalizes the individual by building in his mind the habit of negative thinking and then proceeds to solidify this habit into permanency every second of its existence. Positive thoughts are, likewise, woven by time into permanent habits. The term "permanency," of course, refers to the natural life of the individual. In the strict sense of the term, nothing is permanent. Time converts thought-habits into what might be called permanency during the life of the individual.

Q Now I have a better understanding of how time works. What other characteristics has time in connection with the earthly destiny of human beings?

A Time is nature's seasoning influence through which human experience may be ripened into wisdom. People are not born with wisdom, but they are born with the capacity to think, and they may, through the lapse of time, think their way into wisdom.

"People are not born with wisdom, but they are born with the capacity to think, and they may, through the lapse of time, think their way into wisdom."

\+ + + + + + + + + +

I find this one of the most profound statements in this entire book. By using our ability to think and analyzing our experiences in life, whether successes or failures, we can gain wisdom. Can it actually be that simple?

Q Do youths ever possess wisdom?

A Only in very elementary matters. Wisdom comes only through the lapse of time. It cannot be inherited and it cannot be imparted from one person to another except through the lapse of time.

Q Does the lapse of time force an individual to acquire wisdom?

A No! Wisdom comes only to non-drifters who form positive thought-habits as a dominating force in their lives. Drifters and those whose dominating thoughts are negative never acquire wisdom except of a very elementary nature.

Q From what you say, I infer that time is the friend of the person who trains his mind to follow positive thought-habits and the enemy of the person who drifts into negative thought-habits. Is that correct?

A That is precisely true. All people can be classified as drifters and non-drifters. Drifters are always at the mercy of the non-drifters, and time makes this relationship permanent.

Q Do you mean that if I drift along through life, without definite aim or purpose, the non-drifter may become my master, and time only serves to give the non-drifter a stronger and more permanent grip upon me?

A That is stating the truth exactly.

"Wisdom comes only to non-drifters who form positive thought-habits as a dominating force in their lives."

✦ ✦ ✦ ✦ ✦ ✦ ✦ ✦ ✦ ✦

Again I am forced to think about our children. With so much negativity around us due to terrorism and financial strife, what is going to be the long-term impact on our children? We must envelop our children in positive experiences in order to generate positive thoughts in their minds.

Q What is wisdom?

A Wisdom is the ability to relate yourself to nature's laws so as to make them serve you, and the ability to relate yourself to other people so as to gain their harmonious, willing cooperation in helping you to make life yield whatever you demand of it.

Q Then accumulated knowledge is not wisdom?

A Great heavens, no! If knowledge were wisdom, the achievements of science would not have been converted into implements of destruction.

Q What is needed to convert knowledge into wisdom?

A Time plus the desire for wisdom. Wisdom is never thrust upon one. It is acquired, if at all, by positive thinking, through voluntary effort!

Q Is it safe for all people to have knowledge?

A It is never safe for anyone to have extensive knowledge without wisdom.

Q What is the age at which most people who acquire wisdom begin to acquire it?

A The majority of people who acquire wisdom do so after they have passed the age of forty. Prior to that time the majority of people are too busy gathering knowledge and organizing it into plans to spend any effort seeking wisdom.

Q What circumstance of life is most apt to lead one to acquire wisdom?

A Adversity and failure. These are nature's universal languages through which she imparts wisdom to those who are ready to receive it.

Q Do adversity and failure always bring wisdom?

A No, only to those who are ready for wisdom and have voluntarily sought it.

Q What determines one's readiness to receive wisdom?

A Time and the nature of one's thought-habits.

Q Is newly acquired knowledge the same as time-tested knowledge?

A No, knowledge tested through the lapse of time always is superior to that which has been newly acquired. Time gives to knowledge definiteness in both quality and quantity, and dependability. One never can be sure of knowledge that has not been tested.

Q What is dependable knowledge?

A It is knowledge which harmonizes with natural law, which means that it is based upon positive thought.

Q Does time modify and alter the values of knowledge?

A Yes, time modifies and alters all values. That which is accurate knowledge today may become null and void tomorrow because of time's rearrangement of facts and values. Time modifies all human relationships for better or for worse, depending upon the policy through which people relate themselves to one another.

In the realm of thought there is a time when it is proper to sow the seeds of thought, and there is a proper time to reap the harvest of those thoughts, the same as there is a time to sow and a time to reap from the soil of the earth. Without the proper measurement of time between the sowing and the reaping, nature modifies or withholds the rewards of the sowing.

Q Go ahead, now, and describe the last two of the seven principles.

A The next principle is *harmony.*

Throughout nature one may find evidences that all natural law moves in an orderly manner, through the law of harmony. Through the operation of this law nature forces everything within the range of a given environment to become harmoniously related. Understand this truth and you will catch a new and a more intriguing vision of the power of environment. You will understand why association with negative minds is fatal to those seeking self-determination.

Q Do you mean that nature voluntarily forces human beings to harmonize with the influences of their environment?

A Yes, that is true. The law of hypnotic rhythm forces upon every living thing the dominating influences of the environment in which it exists.

Q If nature forces human beings to take on the nature of the environment in which they live, what means of escape are available to people who find themselves in an environment of poverty and failure but desire to escape?

A They must change their environment or remain poverty-stricken. Nature permits no one to escape the influences of his environment.

However, nature, in her abundance of wisdom, has given to every normal human being the privilege of establishing his own mental, spiritual, and physical environment, but once he establishes it he must become a part of it. This is the inexorable working of the law of harmony.

Q In a business association, for example, who establishes the dominating influence that determines the rhythm of the environment?

A The individual or individuals who think and act with definiteness of purpose.

Q Is it as simple as that?

A Yes, definiteness of purpose is the starting point from which an individual may establish his own environment.

Q I do not seem to follow your reasoning. The entire world is torn with warfare and business depressions and other forms of strife which represent about everything except harmony. Nature does not seem to be forcing people to harmonize with one another. How do you explain this inconsistency?

As in Hill's day, there seems to be little harmony in our world today. When you think of the current economy, the natural disasters, the military conflicts, the human devastation from disease and hunger, does harmony seem even attainable? Hill would say, yes, even in the face of the horrible conditions of his time. While you and I may not be in control of harmony in our world, we can create harmony in our homes.

A There is no inconsistency. The dominating influences of the world are, as you say, negative. Very well, nature is forcing human beings to harmonize with the dominating influences of the world environment.

Manifestations of harmony may be either positive or negative. For example, a group of men in prison may, and they generally do, think and act in a negative manner, but nature sees to it that the dominating influence of the prison is impressed upon every individual in it. A group of poverty-stricken people in a tenement house may fight among themselves and apparently resist all forms of harmony, but nature forces each of them to become a part of the dominating influence of the house in which they live.

Harmony, in the sense it is here used, means that nature relates everything throughout the universes to every other thing of a similar nature. Negative influences are forced into association with one another, no matter where they may be. Positive influences are just as definitely forced into association with one another.

Q I am beginning to see why successful business leaders are so careful in the choice of their business associates. Men who succeed in any calling usually establish their own environment by surrounding themselves with people who think and act in terms of success. Is that the idea?

A That is the idea exactly. Observe, with profit, that the one thing all successful men insist upon is harmony among their business associates. Another trait of successful people is that they move with definiteness of purpose and insist upon their associates doing the same. Understand these two truths and you understand the major difference between a Henry Ford and a day laborer.

So the principle of harmony is a benefit to us when we surround ourselves with other successful people. Think of the people you work with. Are they supporting you . . . or holding you back?

Q Now tell me about the last of the seven principles.

A The last principle is *caution.*

Next to the habit of drifting, the most dangerous human trait is the lack of caution.

People drift into all sorts of hazardous circumstances because they do not exercise caution by planning the moves they make. The drifter always moves without exercising caution. He acts first and thinks later, if at all. He does not choose his friends. He drifts along and allows people to attach themselves to him on their own terms. He does not choose an occupation. He drifts through school and is glad to get the first job that will give him food and clothing. He invites people to cheat him at trade by neglecting to inform himself of the rules of trade. He invites illness by neglecting to inform himself of the rules of sound health. He invites poverty by neglecting to protect himself against the environmental influences of the poverty-stricken. He invites failure at every step he takes by neglecting to exercise the caution to observe what causes people to fail. He invites fear in all its forms by his lack of caution in examining the causes of fear. He fails in marriage because he neglects to use caution in his choice of a mate, and he uses still less caution in his methods of relating himself to her after marriage. He loses his friends or converts them into enemies by his lack of caution in relating himself to them on the proper basis.

"Next to the habit of drifting, the most dangerous human trait is the lack of caution."

Q Are all people lacking in caution?

A No, only those who have acquired the habit of drifting. The non-drifter always uses caution. He carefully thinks his plans through before he begins them. He makes allowances for the human frailties of his associates and plans ahead to bridge them.

If he sends a messenger on an important mission, he sends someone else to make sure the messenger does not neglect his mission. Then he checks on both of them to be sure his wishes have been fulfilled. He takes nothing for granted where caution provides a way to insure his success.

Q Isn't over-caution as detrimental as lack of caution?

A There is no such thing as over-caution. What you call "over-caution" is an expression of fear. Fear and caution are two entirely different things.

Q Don't people mistake fear for over-caution?

A Yes, that does sometimes happen, but the majority of people create for themselves far more disastrous hazards by total lack of the habit of caution than by over-caution.

Q In what way may caution be used most advantageously?

A In the selection of one's associates and in one's method of relating oneself to associates. The reason for this is obvious.

One's associates constitute the most important part of one's environment, and environmental influences determine whether one forms the habit of drifting or becomes a non-drifter. The person who exercises due caution in the choice of associates never allows himself to be closely associated with any person who does not bring to him, through the association, some definite mental, spiritual, or economic benefit.

Q Isn't that method of choosing associates selfish?

A It is sensible and leads to self-determination. It is the desire of every normal person to find material success and happiness.

Nothing contributes more to one's success and happiness than carefully chosen associates. Caution in the selection of associates becomes, therefore, the duty of every person who wishes to become happy and successful. The drifter allows his closest associates to attach themselves to him on their own terms. The non-drifter carefully selects his associates and allows no one to become closely associated with him unless that person contributes some form of helpful influence or bestows some definite benefit.

Q It never occurred to me that caution in the selection of friends had so definite a bearing on one's success or failure. Do all successful people exercise caution in the selection of all their associates, whether in business, social, or professional relationships?

A Without the exercise of caution in the choice of all associates, no one may be certain of success in any calling. On the other hand, lack of exercise of caution brings almost certain defeat in whatever one undertakes.

Do you have a hard time saying "no" to people? This chapter makes you realize that using caution in selecting your associates and learning to say "no" more often may speed you on your path to success.

SUMMARY

THREE THINGS connected with my interview with the Devil interest me most. These three factors interest me because they have been the most important influences in my own life, a fact which any reader of my story can easily discern. The three important factors are the habit of drifting, the law of hypnotic rhythm through which all habits are made permanent, and the element of time.

Here is a trio of forces which hold inviolate the destinies of all men. The three take on a new and more important meaning when they are grouped and studied as a combined force. It takes but little imagination and scarcely any understanding of natural laws for one to see that most of the difficulties in which people find themselves are of their own making. Moreover, difficulties seldom are the outgrowth of immediate circumstances. They are generally the climax of a series of circumstances which have been consolidated through the habit of drifting and with the aid of time.

"Most of the difficulties in which people find themselves are of their own making."

Many people today have a victim mentality which they use as an excuse to not take responsibility for their own lives.

Samuel Insull did not lose his $4 billion industrial empire as the result of the depression. He began losing it long before the depression when he became the victim of a group of women who flattered him into turning his talents from public utilities to grand opera. If ever a man in a high position in the financial world went down because of the power of drifting, hypnotic rhythm, and time, that man was Samuel Insull. I am writing from accurate knowledge of Mr. Insull and the cause of his troubles dating from the time that I served with him during the World War to the time of his ill-advised attempt to run away from himself.

Samuel Insull moved from England to the U.S. in 1881 to become the private secretary of Thomas Edison and rose to become president of the Chicago Edison Co. in 1892. By 1907 he had taken control of Chicago's transit system. By 1912 he was operating several hundred power plants. He vigorously promoted the stock of his holding companies. When they collapsed in 1932, he fled to Europe; extradited in 1934, he was tried three times for fraud, violation of bankruptcy laws, and embezzlement, but was acquitted each time. Hill gives us an inside look at the other reasons for his collapse and fall from grace. Today you instantly know the name Edison...but probably do not recognize Insull.

Henry Ford went through the same depression that swept Mr. Insull under, but Ford came out on top without a scratch. Do you want to know the reason? I'll tell you. Ford has the habit of not drifting on any subject. Time is Ford's friend because he has formed the habit of using it in a positive, constructive manner, with the aid of thoughts of his own making, woven into plans of his own creation.

Take any circumstance you wish, measure it with reference to its relationship to the habit of drifting, hypnotic rhythm, and time, and you may ascertain accurately the cause of all success and all failure.

Franklin D. Roosevelt went into office with a bang during his first term. He had but one major purpose in mind and that was very definite. It was to stop the stampede of fear and start people to thinking and talking in terms of business recovery instead of business depression.

In carrying out that purpose, there was no drifting. The forces of the entire nation were consolidated and moved as one to help carry out the President's definite purpose. For the first time in the history of America, the newspapers of all political leanings, the churches of all denominations, the people of all races and colors, and the political organizations of all brands united themselves into one stupendous power for the sole purpose of helping the President restore faith and normal business relationships in the country.

In a conference held between the President and a group of emergency advisers a few days after he went into office, I asked him what was his major problem. He replied, "It is not a question of majors and minors; we have but one problem and that is to stop fear and supplant it with faith."

Before the end of his first year in office, the President had stopped fear and supplanted it by faith, and the nation was slowly but surely on the way out of the jungle of depression. By the end of his first term—mark well the element of lapse of time—the President had so effectively consolidated the forces of American business and private life that he had an entire nation in back of him, ready, willing, and enthusiastically desirous of following his lead no matter which way he went.

These are facts well known to everyone who reads newspapers or listens to the radio.

Like all of us, Napoleon Hill lived in a political environment that affected everyone. We often think of ourselves as "victims" of the media or the political system or other outside forces. Hill is showing us how to rise above victimhood—another of the Devil's tools—and take responsibility for all our choices.

Then came another presidential election and the opportunity for the people to express their faith in their leader. They expressed it in a landslide without precedent in American politics, and the President went into office a second time with an almost unanimous electorate vote with only two states meekly dissenting.

Now observe how the Wheel of Life began to reverse itself and turn back in the other direction. The President changed his policy from definiteness of purpose to indefiniteness and drifting.

His change of policy split the powerful labor group and turned more than half of it against him. It split the almost-solid following he held in both houses of Congress, and more important than all this, it split the American people into "pro" and "anti" groups with the result that about all the President had left of his original political assets was his million-dollar smile and his ready handshake—obviously not enough to enable him to regain the power he once wielded in American life.

Here, then, we have an excellent example of a man who skyrocketed to great power through definiteness of purpose and belly-flopped to the starting point by his habit of drifting. In both his rise and his fall can be seen clearly the operation of the principles of drifting and non-drifting reaching a climax through the power of hypnotic rhythm and time.

"Here, then, we have an excellent example of a man who skyrocketed to great power through definiteness of purpose and belly-flopped to the starting point by his habit of drifting."

✦ ✦ ✦ ✦ ✦ ✦ ✦ ✦ ✦ ✦

Take a moment to think of other people, in the public eye or in your circle of influence, who achieved great success only to lose it later because of drifting.

All my life the Devil had a dramatic story to tell of his dealings with me. He saw me drift in and out of scores of business opportunities for which many would have given a king's ransom. He saw me drifting in my policy of relating myself to others, particularly in my lack of caution in business dealings.

The circumstance which saved me from fatal control of the law of hypnotic rhythm was the definiteness of purpose with which, at long last, I dedicated my entire life to the organization of a philosophy of individual achievement. I drifted at one time or another on all my minor whims and endeavors, but my drifting was offset by my major purpose, which was sufficient to restore my courage and start me once more in the quest of knowledge every time I was defeated in connection with my minor aims.

I learned something of the hazardous nature of the habit of drifting while engaged in analyzing more than 25,000 people in connection with the organization of the Law of Success. These analyses showed that only two out of every 100 have a definite major aim in life. The other 98 were caught by the habit of drifting. It seems more than a coincidence that my analyses clearly corroborated the Devil's claim that he controls 98 out of every 100 people because of their habit of drifting.

Looking back over my own career, I can see clearly that I could have avoided the majority of the temporary defeats with which I met if I had been definitely following a plan for the attainment of my major purpose in life.

From my experience in having analyzed the problems of more than 5,000 families, I know, definitely, that the majority of married people who get out of harmony with each other do so because of the accumulation of a great number of little circumstances in their married relationship which could have been cleared up and disposed of as they arose if there had been a definite policy to do so. They do not live their married life with definiteness of purpose.

So the story has gone, all back down the ages. The man with the most definite plan and purpose and the most power rides on to victory. The others scurry for cover and get crushed under the heels of those who are more determined.

The answer is not hard to find. There is no use looking toward high heaven for it. For my part I would prefer to seek the answer from the Devil, for he would tell me quickly enough that victory goes to the people who know what they want and are determined to have it. They have mastered the habit of drifting. They have definite policies, definite plans, and definite objectives. Their opposition, which may outnumber them very greatly, has no chance against them because the opposition has no plan, no purpose, no policy except that of drifting along, hoping that something may turn up to help them. In those three brief sentences you have the sum and the substance of the difference between success and failure, power and lack of it.

We come, now, near to the end of our visit through this book. If we were to try to state in one brief sentence the most important part of that which I have tried to convey through the book, it would be something like this:

One's dominating desires can be crystallized into their physical equivalents through definiteness of purpose backed by definiteness of plans, with the aid of nature's law of hypnotic rhythm and time!

There you have the positive phase of the philosophy of individual achievement I have tried to describe through this book, brought down to an irreducible minimum of brevity and simplicity. If you expand the philosophy for the purpose of adapting it to the circumstances of life, you find that it is as broad as life itself, that it covers all human relationships, all human thoughts, aims, and desires.

So here we are, at the end of the strangest of all the thousands of interviews I have had with the great and the near-great, over a period of fifty years of labor, in my search for the truths of life that lead to happiness and economic security.

How strange, indeed, that after having had active cooperation from such men as Carnegie, Edison, and Ford, I should have been compelled, finally, to go to the Devil for a working knowledge of the greatest of all the principles uncovered in my quest for truth. How strange that I was forced to experience poverty and failure and adversity in a hundred forms before being given the privilege of understanding and using a law of nature which softens the thrust of these wicked weapons or wipes them out altogether. But the strangest of all this dramatic experience which life has provided me is the simplicity of the law through which, if I had understood it, I could have transmuted my desires into substantial form without having to undergo so many years of hardship and misery.

I find now, at the end of my interview with the Devil, that I had been carrying in my own pockets the matches with which the fires of adversity were being touched off. And I find, too, that the water with which those fires were finally extinguished was at my command in great abundance.

I searched for the philosopher's lodestone with which failure may be converted into success, only to learn that both success and failure are the results of day-to-day evolutionary forces through which dominating thoughts are pieced together bit by bit and woven into the things we want or the things we do not want, according to the nature of those thoughts.

How unfortunate that I did not understand this truth from the time that I reached the age of reason, for if I had understood it then I might have been able to go around some of the hurdles I have been forced to jump as I walked through "The Valley of the Shadow" of life.

The story of my interview with the Devil is now in your hands. The benefits you will receive from it will be in exact proportion to the thought it inspires in you. To benefit from reading the interview, you need not agree with every portion of it.

You have only to think and to reach your own conclusions concerning every part of it. How reasonable that is. You are the judge and the jury and the attorney for both the prosecution and the defense. If you do not win your case, the loss and the cause thereof will be yours!

—NAPOLEON HILL

"One's dominating desires can be crystallized into their physical equivalents through definiteness of purpose backed by definiteness of plans, with the aid of nature's law of hypnotic rhythm and time!"

Napoleon Hill wanted to share this message with the world in the 1930s, but instead it was hidden away in a vault, to be finally uncovered and shared with you now in 2011—for a reason. *Will you . . .*

- **Realize you are carrying in your own pockets the matches with which the fires of adversity are being touched off, and find, too, that the water with which those fires can be finally extinguished is at your own command in great abundance? And then:**
- **Find your definiteness of purpose?**
- **Create a definite plan?**
- **Engage the aid of nature's law of hypnotic rhythm?**
- **And use the asset of time to assist you in reaching your greatest success?**

AFTERWORD

WHETHER YOU HAVE READ this entire book or only a few of its pages before turning to this afterword, you will have realized that if the historical names, dates, and events in this book were replaced by those of our current times, little has changed. From Hill's description of media propaganda, the conditioning that children receive in school, the fear-based teachings preached by religions, people's poor diet and health habits, to the challenging economic climate, little seems to have shifted in our collective consciousness and therefore in our collective experience.

The good news is that it is never too late for a new beginning, for a renaissance in consciousness. As Mr. Hill reminds us, "I have also discovered that there comes with every experience of temporary defeat, and every failure and every form of adversity, the seed of an equivalent benefit." Our path is seemingly composed of a polarity of both failure and success. A lighter way of putting it might be that Hill's principles for living teach us "how to fail successfully." This is a paradox understood by the spiritually mature, those whom he describes as having risen above the "hypnotic rhythm" and discovered their "other self," which can also be identified as the Self of the self, the Higher Self, or the Authentic Self.

It is encouraging that many of today's spiritual, philosophical, self-help, and even scientific authors share Hill's view of what he calls "definiteness of purpose," or, in current parlance, "intention setting." When it is our intention to wake up from the "hypnotic rhythm" of living—what the Hindus call delusion and the Buddhists call illusion—individual and collective consciousness expands. We, along with our global family, benefit.

Hill's integrity shines through his descriptions of what it means to manifest success. In fact, he unhesitatingly announces that "any man can avail himself of the benefits of his 'other self'" as long as he is not "steeped in greed." This spiritually dignified statement elevates success to a matter of consciousness—that is, success does not necessarily mean that "he who has the most toys wins." Hill thus eliminates confusing spiritual awakening with the capacity to manifest things in one's life, for there is never enough of "more."

We are also taught the importance of awareness, of mindfulness, an activity of consciousness abhorred by Hill's Devil, who delights in using people's lack of thinking for themselves to his advantage. Consciously observing the mind and its capacities is to look at it with respect, compassion, gratitude, for it is God's gift to us. Mind not only forms our inner landscape; it creates our outer circumstances. Let us not fight with the mind; let us appreciate its nuances, its intuitions, its utmost capacities with the understanding that mind is the key to being self-directed, self-empowered, self-confident.

Next to "drifting," the most dangerous human trait Hill describes is the "lack of caution," or what we might call a lack of discernment. Discernment is a relative of wisdom, which causes us to think of the repercussions before we take action, as well as to honestly observe the results of our choice-making. Thus we may create our own path to freedom.

In the minds of his modern-day readers, Hill's teachings are most often associated with prosperity, which translates as money in one's individual coffers. But truth be told, he has shared with the world his wisdom of "how-to-live principles," beginning with one's interior being, one's inner state of consciousness, inviting us to give outer expression to our highest potential not only for our own benefit, but for all humankind.

I wish to add that it was a wisdom-guided choice on the part of the Napoleon Hill Foundation to entrust this precious manuscript to the able hands of Sharon Lechter. Her many years of deeply studying Napoleon Hill's truth principles, and more importantly her practice of them, have made her a perfect candidate to now offer this manuscript to the world.

May all Hill's readers break free from conditional belief systems and live life in all of its richness, its exquisite beauty and joy, freely delivering their gifts, talents, and skills on this planet we all call home. Peace and richest blessings to you!

—MICHAEL BERNARD BECKWITH

MICHAEL BERNARD BECKWITH is the author of *Spiritual Liberation: Fulfilling Your Soul's Potential*, and was featured in *The Secret.* He is the founder of the Agape International Spiritual Center and the co-founder of the Association for Global New Thought, and the Season for Nonviolence.

IN REFLECTION

THROUGHOUT NAPOLEON HILL'S WRITINGS, there is a strong spirituality present, informing his methods and his morality. In many places in the present book, *Outwitting the Devil*, this religious foundation for his belief system is perhaps at its most explicit.

Some of his statements about evil and fear, about "indefiniteness" and "drifting," derive from an American religious tradition that dates back, at least, to the Transcendentalism of Ralph Waldo Emerson in the mid-nineteenth century. Currents in American spirituality in Hill's day (during the writing of this book in the late 1930s) included Norman Vincent Peale, Emmett Fox, and, in popular inspirational fiction, Lloyd C. Douglas. The very personal Christian evangelism of Aimee Semple McPherson and Billy Sunday were also still omnipresent in the media and public consciousness of the era.

For Hill, however, the stature of some of the titans of industry and finance of the time achieved a kind of religious validation and served to inspire his own thought and action, and he urged others to look to these men—and all were men—as models of successful moral behavior that yielded personal success as well as general good.

The Great Depression was, for Napoleon Hill, in great measure a moral failure. What would he say about our current crises in financial markets—the near collapse of the banking system in 2008 and the subsequent severe recession that has affected the lives of everyone who will pick up this book in 2011 and beyond?

His pantheon included Carnegie (of course), Edison, Ford, and Rockefeller. Each of these tycoons has been subsequently analyzed and reanalyzed by historians, economists, and biographers and their personal flaws placed in the glare of public scrutiny. To Hill, they were not historical figures but contemporary leaders on the world stage—as were Adolf Hitler and Benito Mussolini, Franklin Roosevelt and Winston Churchill. He did not critique Rockefeller's ruthless competitiveness, and he was probably unaware at the time of Ford's anti-Semitism.

For Hill, American society and the free market system held the best hope for the world as it teetered on the brink of conflagration—and even with the evident imperfections of his native country (what he saw as its susceptibility to the Devil's machinations), there was nothing on earth that could compare with it.

For individuals who made the personal choice to succeed in life, who resisted the temptations and weaknesses of irreligion and sought, instead, the help of God (called by various names in the book), there was no limit to how far they might go. Limits were self-imposed, or imposed by the negative outside force of evil, personified by the Devil.

So what is Hill's religion? Frankly, that is not important to me. As much as I have been influenced by Napoleon Hill's philosophy and fascinated by his life, it has never mattered to me what church he attended or whether he attended any church at all. More important is the question: What is he teaching us today about the role of faith in our lives?

The answer to that question is for you to decide. I think it is a foundational issue that affects every line he writes. After all, he chose to frame this book in the classical genre of the philosophical dialogue, and he sets up a sparring match with the most vivid anti-religious figure in all of literature (from the Bible, through Milton, through C.S. Lewis). And I continue to be fascinated by this choice for it allows Hill to express—in a very readable style—his own deeply held beliefs and theories about human behavior. It holds profound lessons for us all.

As you go forward in your life and find obstacles in your way, it may serve you to review Hill's seven principles for *Outwitting the Devil* in your life.

- *Definiteness of purpose*
- *Mastery over self*
- *Learning from adversity*
- *Controlling environmental influence (associations)*
- *Time (giving permanency to positive, rather than negative thought-habits and developing wisdom)*
- *Harmony (acting with definiteness of purpose to become the dominating influence in your own mental, spiritual, and physical environment)*
- *Caution (thinking through your plan before you act)*

In reviewing these seven principles, you may identify and reveal what is holding you back from achieving your greatest success.

It was a profound blessing to me to have the Napoleon Hill Foundation entrust this manuscript to my hands—a manuscript that was hidden and locked away for over seventy years (either by his wife or the Devil himself... you decide). They say when a student is ready, the teacher will appear. Is it possible that *Think and Grow Rich* was the right message during the

Great Depression and that *Outwitting the Devil* is the right message for our current times? I believe we see God's hand at work, not the Devil's. I believe *Outwitting the Devil* was not published until God felt it was the right message at the right time . . . now for us in 2011. It has definitely made a huge impact in my life and I hope that you will find value in it for your life.

May Napoleon Hill's words bring you
hope, courage, and, most of all,
definiteness of purpose for your life . . .
Be blessed.

—Sharon Lechter

ACKNOWLEDGMENTS

A TREMENDOUS NUMBER of people have played a role in bringing *Outwitting the Devil* to print after it spent more than seventy years in hiding.

The Napoleon Hill Foundation deeply appreciates the family of Dr. Napoleon Hill, who have kept his legacy alive. Dr. Charlie Johnson, Hill's nephew, who had custody of the controversial manuscript, recognized the power and relevance of its message and recently gave the manuscript to the Napoleon Hill Foundation so it could be published.

Many thanks to Sharon Lechter and her deep passion for preserving and promoting Hill's legacy. In her comments throughout the book, Sharon has used her talents and energy to help readers appreciate and benefit from this timely message.

Sharon joins us in thanking the admirers of Napoleon Hill all over the world who help us spread Hill's wisdom—teachers and mentors, motivational speakers and college professors, successful business leaders and budding entrepreneurs. You are living testaments to the continued importance of Hill's work. Little wonder that Hill was often introduced as Miracle Maker and Maker of Millionaires during the many years of his speaking tours.

We thank the entire team at Sterling Publishing for their dedication and expertise, most notably Marcus Leaver, Jason Prince, Michael Fragnito, and Kate Zimmermann. On a more personal note, we thank our teams at The Napoleon Hill Foundation and Pay Your Family First for their never-ending guidance and support . . . Robert T. Johnson Jr., Michael Lechter, Annedia Sturgill, Phillip Lechter, Kevin Stock, Angela Totman, and Kristin Thomas. In addition, we appreciate the encouragement and assistance from Steve Riggio, Greg Reid, Joe McNeely, Greg Tobin, and Cevin Bryerman.

On behalf of Napoleon Hill, whose journey began over a century ago and whose wisdom has brought hope and encouragement to millions of people around the globe, we thank you!

—DON GREEN, CEO of the Napoleon Hill Foundation,
and SHARON LECHTER

NAPOLEON HILL

1883–1970

NAPOLEON HILL WAS BORN IN 1883 in the remote mountains of Wise County, Virginia. He was born into poverty, and his mother died when he was nine years old. One year later his father remarried, and his stepmother became a source of inspiration for the young boy.

With the influence of his stepmother, Hill became a newspaper reporter while in his teens. His writings got the attention of Robert L. Taylor, former governor of Tennessee and later a United States senator. Taylor owned *Bob Taylor's Magazine* and employed the young Hill to write success stories. At the time, Hill was enrolled at Georgetown University Law School.

In 1908 Hill was assigned to interview Andrew Carnegie and a three-hour interview became one that lasted three days. While Hill did the interviewing, Carnegie sold him on the idea of organizing the world's first philosophy of personal achievement, based on the principles of success.

Carnegie provided Hill with introductions to giants of the time including Henry Ford, Thomas A. Edison, and John D. Rockefeller. Hill was to spend twenty years interviewing, studying, and writing about successful individuals.

It would be twenty years after Hill interviewed Andrew Carnegie before he wrote the eight-volume *Law of Success* in 1928. He was to write many best sellers in his lifetime. In 1937 Hill wrote *Think and Grow Rich*, which became the best-selling self-help book of all time and continues today to sell millions of copies all over the world. Little wonder that Hill was often introduced as Miracle Man—Maker of Millionaires.

SHARON LECHTER

A LIFE-LONG EDUCATION ADVOCATE, Sharon Lechter is the founder of Pay Your Family First, a financial education organization. Sharon serves as a national spokesperson for the National CPA Financial Literacy Commission. In 2008 Sharon was appointed to the first President's Advisory Council on Financial Literacy, serving both Presidents Bush and Obama.

Sharon is an entrepreneur, author, philanthropist, educator, international speaker, licensed CPA, and mother. She has been a pioneer in developing new technologies, programs, and products to bring education into children's lives in ways that are innovative, challenging, and fun. Her financial literacy board game, ThriveTime for Teens, an innovative and experiential life and money reality game, has gained recognition with coveted awards including the GOLD Mom's Choice Award, *Creative Child Magazine's* 2010 Game of The Year, Dr. Toy's Best Vacation Product, and a five-star rating from WTS Toy Reviews. Sharon is recognized as an expert on the topics of financial education for children, personal finance, and entrepreneurship.

Sharon authored the national best seller *Three Feet from Gold* in cooperation with the Napoleon Hill Foundation and Greg Reid. Sharon is also known world-wide as the co-author of the international #1 *New York Times* best seller *Rich Dad Poor Dad* and fourteen other books in the *Rich Dad* series.

A committed philanthropist, Sharon also gives back to world communities as both a volunteer and benefactor. Sharon serves on the national boards of the Women Presidents' Organization, and Childhelp, a national organization founded to prevent and treat child abuse.

www.sharonlechter.com · www.payyourfamilyfirst.com · www.outwittingthedevil.com

INDEX

Achievement
- emergencies and, 24
- failure and, 2, 106
- faith and, 47–49
- happiness and, xv
- Hill lecturing on, 15, 18, 22
- principles of, 7, 11
- relationships and, 224
- success and, 2
- teaching, 2–3

Adversity. *See also* Failure(s)
- advantages from, 53, 202, 217
- benefits of, 213–214
- blessing of, 14
- change with, 5
- learning from, 148, 202
- in relationships, 212–213
- wisdom from, 234

America Saves, 181
Attraction, 118, 132–133, 140, 144

Bell, Alexander Graham, 3
Betsy Ross Candy Company, 7
Brain(s)
- choosing negative or positive thoughts, 137
- combining, 130
- constant motion of, 227
- desires and, 225
- evolution of, 228–229
- food and, 187, 188
- Infinite Intelligence and, 117, 176, 228
- "other self" and, 214
- senses and, 210
- sixth sense and, 211
- thought process in, 209–210, 225
- unused portions of, 60, 72
- weak, 74

Bribery, 111–112, 115, 116, 129, 137, 150, 154
Bryant & Stratton Business College, 8

Carnegie, Andrew, 2–5, 12, 17, 19, 22, 54, 256
Caution, 239–241
Children
- definiteness of purpose and, 151–152, 168–169
- drifting of, 75, 79, 163, 177
- duty and, 163
- fear affecting, 78, 80, 151
- habits and, 175
- hypnotic rhythm and, 151
- mind of, 75–83
- parents teaching, 79, 151
- positive thoughts for, 233
- religion for, 77–78, 151
- schools and. *See* Schools
- using independent thinking, 77–79, 81–82, 83, 143, 151

Cigarettes, 64, 65–66, 177
Compensation, law of, 41, 153, 157, 177, 217
Confucius, 63
Criticism, 126, 127

Death, 61, 63, 124–125
Declaration of Independence, 87
Desire(s)
- attainment of, 43
- brains and, 225
- bribery and, 112, 116
- habits from, 225
- hypnotic rhythm and, 225
- Infinite Intelligence and, 117
- for money, 113
- negative, 226
- "other self" assisting, 29

for sex, 111, 129
thoughts and, 225–226
Dictatorships, 87–88, 108
Doubt, 5, 14, 29, 45. *See also* Indecision
Drifting
accurate thoughts and, 84
attraction and, 133
bribery affecting, 116
caution and, 239, 240
of children, 75, 79, 163, 177
definiteness of purpose and, 149, 150, 223
description of, 91–93
dictators and, 87
environments and, 85, 223
failure and, 89, 104, 245
faith and, 184
flattery affecting, 101–102
Ford ignoring, 244
Franklin D. Roosevelt and, 88, 245, 246
habits and, 153
Hill, 247–248
hypnotic rhythm and, 131, 142, 243, 244
independent thinking and, 95, 116
laws of nature and, 86
losing soul through, 122–123
marriage and, 84, 161
of mind, 73–75, 86, 99
money and, 89–90
occupations and, 84–85
opinions and, 194
opportunities and, 135
overcoming, 118, 131
parents teaching, 79
poverty and, 89, 183
prayer affecting, 164–165
religion promoting, 170–171
schools promoting, 170–171
self-determination and, 83, 183
thoughts and, 73–75, 99
time and, 243, 244
wisdom and, 232
Duty, 161–163, 224
Edison, Thomas, 3, 39, 47, 105, 166, 244
Education. *See* Schools
Egotism, 102–104, 111, 153, 195, 213
Emergencies
achievement and, 24
fear and, 17, 18, 19, 20
indecision and, 18
"other self" and, 5, 21–22
Emerson, Ralph Waldo, 41, 63, 177
Emotions, 67, 210
Environment(s)
changing, 236
definiteness of purpose and, 237
drifting and, 85, 223
habits and, 75
harmony and, 236
human relationships and, 220–221, 223, 224
hypnotic rhythm and, 145, 220, 222
influence of, 27, 28, 145, 224
vibration of, 131

Failure(s). *See also* Adversity
achievement and, 106
blessing of, 37–41, 202, 214
Carnegie on, 2–5
causes of, 2, 5, 7
caution and, 239
definiteness of purpose and, 155–157
drifting and, 89, 104, 245
of Edison, 47
hypnotic rhythm and, 202, 204–205, 206, 215, 245
learning from, 4, 105, 117
"other self" and, 36, 214
quitting after, 202
time and, 245
virtue of, 106, 163
wisdom from, 234
Faith
achievement and, 47–49
affecting fear, 46
drifting and, 184

Franklin D. Roosevelt and, 245
God and, 49
"other self" and, 27, 28, 38
as sixth sense, 49
Fear
affecting children, 78, 80, 151
causing Great Depression, 229
caution and, 239, 240
of criticism, 126, 127
of death, 61, 124–125
definiteness of purpose and, 154
emergencies and, 17, 18, 19, 20
faith affecting, 46
Franklin D. Roosevelt and, 245
of hell, 78
hypnotic rhythm and, 124–125
impeding prayer, 43
mass, 68, 229–230
mind and, 61
"other self" and, 27–28, 45
overcoming, 23, 100
paralyzing effect of, 17–19, 20
of poverty, 61, 85, 112
propaganda in, 109
religion using, 80, 83, 125, 142, 151
salvation from, 171
as sin, 183
Finances. *See* Money
Flattery, 100–104, 129, 141
Food
definiteness of purpose and, 188
illness and, 188
over-indulgence of, 84, 112, 113, 114, 187–188
self-discipline with, 186–189
waste elimination and, 189
Ford, Henry, 3, 105, 244

Gandhi, 162
Gillette, King, 3
Gluttony, 113
God. *See also* Infinite Intelligence
description of, 49
flattering, 141
power of mind and, 123, 140
prayers to, 43, 164
as source, 57
Golden Rule magazine, 8, 9, 132
Gratitude, 44–45
Gravitation, law of, 121
Great Depression, 37, 40, 46, 52, 68, 135–136, 206, 229
Green, Don, xi-xiii, 27, 227

Habit(s)
changing, 5, 22, 118, 223
children and, 175
cigarette, 64, 65–66
contagious, 196
definiteness of purpose and, 153
from desires, 225
drifting and, 73–75, 153, 223
environments and, 75
Great Depression affecting, 135
independent thinking and, 77–78
permanence of, 231
rhythm of, 122
of sex, 190
thoughts and, 224–225
Happiness, 160–161
achievement and, xv
money and, 9–10
through service, 13, 42, 162
Harmony, 236–239, 248
Henley, William Ernest, 22–23
Heredity, 74, 145, 151
Hill, Annie Lou, xi, xii
Hill, Napoleon
death of, 98, 127
definiteness of purpose and, 247
drifting, 247–248
during Great Depression, 52
interviewing Carnegie, 2–5
jobs of, 7–9
Law of Success by, 3
as lecturer, 15, 18, 22
as publisher, 8, 9
Think and Grow Rich by, xii, 3–4, 5
wife of, xi, xii, 127, 130
Hitler, Adolf, 87–88
Hypnotic rhythm
attraction and, 132, 144

character and, 206
children and, 151
description of, 120–121
desires and, 225
drifting and, 131, 142, 243, 244
environments and, 145, 220, 222
failure and, 202, 203–205, 206, 215, 245
fear and, 124–125
human relationships and, 207–209
influence of, 136–137
as law of compensation, 217
laws of nature and, 120–121, 131–132, 203, 249
marriage and, 207
permanence of, 222, 231
poverty and, 144, 207
prayer and, 164
success and, 144, 207, 245
time and, 230, 243, 244

Illness, 63, 64, 84, 89, 182, 188
Indecision, 11, 17, 18, 45, 53. *See also* Doubt
Independent thinking. *See also* Thoughts
children using, 77–79, 81–82, 83, 143, 151
definiteness of purpose and, 171
drifting and, 95, 116
habits and, 77–78
Infinite Intelligence and, 140
opinions and, 198
parents and, 77–78, 79, 151
religion and, 77–78, 79, 83, 151
schools and, 77–78, 79, 81–82, 83, 151, 172
Infinite Intelligence. *See also* God
abilities of, 48–49
access to, 228
brains and, 117, 176, 228
desires and, 117
gratitude to, 44
independent thinking and, 140
negativity and, 140
overcoming obstacles and, 39
prayer and, 43, 44
reality of, 130–131
Insull, Samuel, 244
"Invictus" (Henley), 22–23

Junior Achievement, 181

Knowledge, 234, 235
Krone, Julie, 105

LaSalle Extension University of Chicago, 7
Law of Success (Hill), xiii, 3
Lincoln, Abraham, 63
Love, 154–155
Luck, 133–134

Marriage, 84, 161, 207, 221, 222, 239, 248
McDermott, Pat, 15, 16
Mellett, Don R., 15–16, 17, 19
Metropolitan Business College, 14
Mind. *See also* Thoughts
affecting prayer, 48
bribery and, 111
of children, 75–83
Devil controlling, 60–61, 62, 78
drifting of, 73–75, 86, 99
fear and, 61
independent thinking and, 77–78
Master, 54–55, 57, 130, 213, 223
subconscious, 209–210, 211
Money
beliefs affecting, 46
desire for, 113
drifting and, 89–90
happiness and, 9–10
loss of, 215
"other self" and, 24–25, 28, 35–36
problems from, 113–114
success with, 9
Mother Teresa, 162
Mussolini, Benito, 87–88

Napoleon Hill Foundation, 27

Napoleon Hill Magazine, 9
Nature, laws of
  climate and, 143
  drifting and, 86
  eternal change in, 206
  faith and, 28
  harmony and, 236
  hypnotic rhythm and, 120–121, 131–132, 203, 249
  Omnipotence and, 167
  time and, 218
  wisdom and, 233
Newton, Isaac, 121

Opinions, 186, 194–197, 198
"Other self"
  assisting desires, 29
  brains and, 214
  doubt and, 45
  emergencies and, 5, 21–22
  emerging, 5, 6, 11
  experience of, 12–13
  failure and, 214
  faith and, 27, 28, 38
  fear and, 27–28, 45
  guidance of, 24–30
  indecision and, 45
  limitations and, 34, 36
  money and, 24–25, 28, 35–36
  prayer and, 48

Paine, Thomas, 63
Parents, 77–78, 79, 151, 163
Pelton, Albert L., 33–34
Politics, 64, 79, 108, 141
Poverty
  caution and, 239
  drifting and, 89, 183
  fear of, 61, 85, 112
  hypnotic rhythm and, 144, 207
  sex and, 189–190
  thoughts and, 63, 64
Powell, Earl, 35
Prayer(s)
  with definiteness of purpose, 163–164, 177
  drifting affecting, 164–165
  fear impeding, 43
  to God, 43, 164
  gratitude in, 44–45
  hypnotic rhythm and, 164
  Infinite Intelligence and, 43
  mind affecting, 48
  "other self" and, 48
  success with, 43, 117, 164
Predestination, 167
Procrastination. *See* Drifting
Propaganda, 107–110, 124
Purpose, definiteness of
  acquiring, 150
  children and, 151–152, 168–169
  danger of, 153
  drifting and, 149, 150, 223
  environments and, 237
  failure and, 155–157
  fear and, 154
  food and, 188
  Franklin D. Roosevelt and, 245, 246
  habits and, 153
  of Hill, 247
  independent thinking and, 171
  losing, 152
  love and, 154–155
  prayer with, 163–164, 177
  religion and, 168–171
  schools and, 172–173
  successful plans with, 155–157, 166

Religion
  for children, 77–78, 151
  definiteness of purpose and, 168–171
  independent thinking and, 77–78, 83
  promoting drifting, 170–171
  propaganda in, 107
  sin and, 182–183
  using fear, 80, 83, 125, 142, 151
Rockefeller, John D., 3, 64, 65
Roosevelt, Franklin D., 88, 245–246
Roosevelt, Theodore, 3

Schools
  definiteness of purpose and, 168–171, 172–173
  illness and, 84
  independent thinking and, 77–78, 79, 81–82, 83, 151, 172
  positive changes for, 174–182
  private, 179–180
  promoting drifting, 170–171
  propaganda in, 107
  teaching practical lessons, 180–181
Science, 127–128, 165–166
Self-determination
  accurate thinking and, 193
  associates and, 241
  caution and, 241
  drifting from, 83, 183
  education and, 172–173
  love and, 155
  negative thoughts and, 224, 236
Self-discipline
  with food, 186–189
  with opinions, 186, 194–197
  with sex, 186, 189–194
Service
  effects of, 95
  happiness through, 13, 42, 162
  priority of, 117
Sex
  accurate thinking and, 193–194
  desire for, 111, 129
  draining energy, 191
  habit of, 190
  over-indulgence of, 66, 113, 186
  positive effects of, 191–192
  poverty and, 189–190
  self-discipline with, 186, 189–194
  women using, 101
Sin, 182–183
Sixth sense, 48, 49, 177, 210, 211, 214
Socrates, 63
Stalin, Joseph, 87–88
Success
  Carnegie on, 2–5
  causes of, 2
  definiteness of purpose and, 155–157
  drifting and, 245
  equation for, 49
  happiness and, 9
  hypnotic rhythm and, 144, 207, 245
  with money, 9
  with prayer, 43, 117, 164
  time and, 245
Success magazine, 9

Teach for America, 181
Team work, 54–55
Think and Grow Rich (Hill), xii, 3–4, 5
Thoughts. *See also* Independent thinking; Mind
  accurate, 80, 83, 84, 166, 193–194, 228
  attraction of, 118, 140
  brain storing, 210
  deeds following, 134
  desires and, 225–226
  drifting and, 73–75, 79, 83, 84, 99
  emotional, 210
  habits and, 224–225
  nature and, 226–228
  negative, 61–62, 75, 85, 121, 220–221, 224, 231
  positive, 64, 216, 221, 231, 233
  poverty and, 63, 64
  rhythm of, 122
  sixth sense and, 210–211
Time, 157, 228, 229, 230–235, 243, 244, 245

Voltaire, 63

Wars, 8, 68, 94, 101, 107, 141, 217
Wisdom, 231–235
World War I, 8, 68

The purpose of The Napoleon Hill Foundation is to…

- *Advance the concept of private enterprise offered under the American System*
- *Teach individuals by formula how they can rise from humble beginnings to positions of leadership in their chosen professions*
- *Assist young men and women to set goals for their own lives and careers*
- *Emphasize the importance of honesty, morality and integrity as the cornerstone of Americanism*
- *Aid in the development of individuals to help them reach their own potential*
- *Overcome the self-imposed limitations of fear, doubt and procrastination*
- *Help people rise from poverty, physical handicaps, and other disadvantages to high positions, wealth and acquire the true riches of life*
- *Motivate individuals to motivate themselves to high achievements*

THE NAPOLEON HILL FOUNDATION
www.naphill.org
www.outwittingthedevil.com

A not-for-profit educational institution dedicated to making the world a better place in which to live.

Please share your personal stories of how you succeeded in Outwitting the Devil.

By visiting *www.outwittingthedevil.com*, you can join our community. Share your own story of how you outwitted the Devil and you will be helping others to realize that they can too!

If you are still fighting the Devil yourself, you will be able to learn how other community members faced their own moments of struggle, what helped them persevere, and how they achieved success.

It may just be the motivation you need, to propel you to success!

Whatever the mind can conceive and believe, it can achieve!

—Napoleon Hill

Sharon Lechter
and
The Napoleon Hill Foundation

www.outwittingthedevil.com · *www.naphill.org*

The Secret Chapter

Unlocked for you today

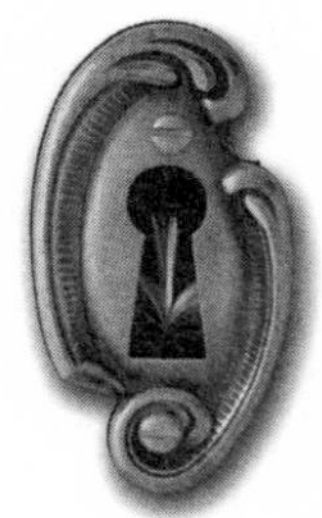

The chapter excluded from the book
is available to you—as our gift!

"An interview with my Invisible Counselors . . .
my Strangest Experience."

—Napoleon Hill

Find more about OUTWITTING THE DEVIL,
the secrets, and the insider details from Sharon Lechter
at OutwittingTheDevil.com

Visit

OutwittingTheDevil.com

to download this amazing chapter

Praise for
OUTWITTING THE DEVIL

"We are told too often to ignore the existence of the negative and to focus only on the positive. Yet the power comes in recognizing both and learning to deal with them. This book tells a great story and teaches some terrific lessons."

—LARRY WINGET, *New York Times* and *Wall Street Journal* best-selling author of *Shut Up, Stop Whining & Get a Life!*

"Napoleon Hill's immortal *Think and Grow Rich* was 50 years ahead of its time. His newly discovered treasure, *Outwitting the Devil,* is further proof of his wisdom and his legacy. Hill guides you through true and false, best and worst, and right and wrong, as if he were alive today. This book is not an option for anyone looking for today's insights that will lead you to tomorrow's success and fulfillment."

—JEFFREY GITOMER, author of *The Little Red Book of Selling* and *The Little Gold Book of YES Attitude*

"If you don't program yourself, life will program you! Napoleon Hill's *Outwitting the Devil* provides you the code to achieve your greatest potential!"

—LES BROWN, The Motivator! author of *Live Your Dreams*

"Hill takes an idea that C. S. Lewis used in *The Screwtape Letters,* expands it, and then presents it in a very personal way. The result is a fascinating look into the mind of Napoleon Hill and how he sees society as blindly programming us for failure. *Outwitting the Devil* may still be too 'hot' to publish."

—DR. J. B. HILL, Napoleon Hill's grandson

"The single greatest look into the mind of the inspirational legend, Napoleon Hill."

—GREG S. REID, co-author of *Three Feet from Gold*

"Hill's teachings are most often associated, in the minds of his modern-day readers, with prosperity, which translates as money in one's individual coffers. But truth be told, he has shared with the world his wisdom of 'how-to-live principles,' beginning with one's interior being, one's inner state of consciousness, inviting us to give outer expression to our highest potential not only for our own benefit, but for all humankind."

—MICHAEL BERNARD BECKWITH,
author of *Spiritual Liberation: Fulfilling Your Soul's Potential*

"Napoleon Hill's ageless wisdom has been combined with Sharon Lechter's ability to communicate with the modern reader in *Outwitting the Devil,* the profound and life-changing sequel to *Think and Grow Rich.* As you read it and then read it again, you will realize that what you think about, you bring about!"

—RITA DAVENPORT, author, speaker, and humorist

"*Think and Grow Rich* revealed the fundamental principles of success ... *Outwitting the Devil* will reveal what may be getting in your way, how to break through those barriers and achieve the success you deserve.

—JIM STOVALL, best-selling author of *The Ultimate Gift*

"You will discover whether the Devil he interviews is real or imaginary, much like the Devil that you may personally be dealing with in your life and experience."

—MARK VICTOR HANSEN, co-creator of the #1 *New York Times*
best-selling series *Chicken Soup for the Soul®*

"There has never been a more important time for truth than now. I am proud of Sharon Lechter's bravery to step forward to put God in the center of our lives."

—SARA O'MEARA, co-founder and chair of Childhelp, Inc.,
five-time nominee for the Nobel Peace Prize